4.90

THE FULL BLESSING OF PENTECOST

THE FULL BLESSING
OF PENTECOST

THE ONE THING NEEDFUL

ANDREW MURRAY

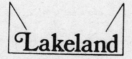

LAKELAND

BLUNDELL HOUSE
GOODWOOD ROAD
LONDON SE14 6BL

This edition   *1954*
Reprinted   *1956*
Reprinted   *1958*
Reprinted   *1960*
Reprinted   *1963*
Reprinted   *1965*
Reprinted   *1968*
Reprinted   *1970*
Reprinted   *1971*
Reprinted   *1972*

ISBN 0 551 00025 2

Printed in Great Britain by Lowe & Brydone (Printers) Ltd.,
London, N.W.10

PREFACE

In all our study of the work of the blessed Spirit, and in all our pursuit of a life in His fulness, we shall ever find the sum of Christ's teaching in those wonderful words: "He that believeth on Me, as the Scripture hath said, out of his belly shall flow rivers of living water." It is as we are convicted of the defectiveness of our faith in Christ, and what He has promised to do in saving and keeping us from sin, and as we understand that believing in Him means a yielding up of the whole heart and life and will, to let Him rule and live within us, that we can confidently count upon receiving all that we need of the Holy Spirit's power and presence. It is as Christ becomes to us all that God has made Him to be, that the Holy Spirit can flow from Him and do His blessed work of leading us back to know Him better and to believe in Him more completely.

My attention has been directed by a brother to the Epistle to the Hebrews, and to the way it speaks of Christ in His heavenly glory and power as the object of our faith. In my book, *The Holiest of All*, I have tried to point out (see chaps. lxv.-lxx., and elsewhere) how the Holy Spirit reveals the way into the Holiest as opened by the blood of Christ, and invites us by faith in Christ to have our life there. It is as we yield our hearts to the leading of the Spirit to know Christ and look at Him, and believe in what is revealed, that the Spirit can take possession of us. The Spirit is given to reveal Christ, and every revelation of Christ fully accepted gives the Spirit room to dwell and work within us. This is the sure way in which the promise will be fulfilled: "He that believeth on Me, rivers of living water shall flow out of him." May God lead us to this simple and full faith in Christ, our great High Priest and King in the heavens, and so into a life in the fulness of the Spirit.   ANDREW MURRAY.

CONTENTS

INTRODUCTION

The message which this little book brings is simple but most solemn. It is to the effect that *the one thing needful for the Church, and the thing which, above all others, men ought everywhere to seek for with one accord and with their whole heart, is to be filled with the Spirit of God.*

In order to secure attention to this message and attract the hearts of my readers to the blessing of which it speaks, I have laid particular emphasis on certain main points. These I briefly state here.

1. *It is the will of God that every one of His children should live entirely and unceasingly under the control of the Holy Spirit.*

2. *Without being filled with the Spirit, it is utterly impossible that an individual Christian or a church can ever live or work as God desires.*

3. *Everywhere and in everything we see the proofs, in the life and experience of Christians, that this blessing is but little enjoyed in the Church, and, alas! is but little sought for.*

4. *This blessing is prepared for us and God waits to bestow it. Our faith may expect it with the greatest confidence.*

5. *The great hindrance in the way is that the self-life, and the world, which it uses for its own service and pleasure, usurp the place that Christ ought to occupy.*

6. *We cannot be filled with the Spirit until we are prepared to yield ourselves to be led by the Lord Jesus to forsake and sacrifice everything for this pearl of great price.*

I feel very deeply the imperfection that attaches to this little volume. Yet I am not without the hope that the Lord will make it a blessing to His people. We have such a feeble conception of the unspiritual and sinful state which prevails in the Church, that, unless we take time to devote our heart and our thoughts to the real facts of the case, the promise of God can make no deep impression upon us. I hope that the attempt I have made to exhibit the subject in various aspects will help to prepare the way for the conviction that this blessing is in truth *the one thing needful*, and that to get possession of *this one thing* we ought to bid farewell to everything else we hold dear. I frankly invite Christian disciples into whose hands the book may fall to peruse it carefully more than once. Owing to the prevailing lack of the presence and operation of the Spirit, it takes a long time ere these spiritual truths concerning the need, and the fulness, and the reality of the Spirit's power can obtain mastery over us. It is only by the exercise of self-sacrifice and persisting in keeping our minds occupied with these thoughts, that we can ever obtain what might otherwise come to us at once.

On reviewing what I have written, I am inclined to think that there is one point on which I ought to have spoken more definitely. I refer to the place which persevering prayer must occupy in connection with this blessing. This little book was not exclusively written for prayer at the season of Pentecost. *Every day ought to be a Pentecostal season in the Church of Christ.* For just as little as a man can remain in sound health without the fresh air of heaven, can Christians or the Church live according to the will of God without this blessing. The book is designed to point to what must prevail throughout all the year; and it seems to me now that, perhaps under the impression that in the season of Pentecost prayer for the blessing is practically unanimous, I have not strongly enough exhorted my readers to ceaseless calling upon God in the confidence that He will answer. Let me advert again to this point in a few sentences.

When we read the Book of the Acts, we see that the filling with the Spirit and His mighty operation was always obtained by prayer. Recall, for example, what took place at Antioch. It was when the Christians there were engaged in fasting and prayer that God regarded them as prepared to receive the revelation that they must separate Barnabas and Saul; and it was only after they had once more fasted and prayed that these two men went forth, sent by the Holy Spirit.[1] These servants of God felt that the boon they needed *must come only from above*. To obtain the blessing we so much need, from heaven and out of the hands of the living God Himself, we in like manner, even with fasting, must liberate ourselves as far as possible from the demands of the earthly life, even in that which otherwise appears quite lawful; and no less must we betake ourselves wholly to God in prayer. Let us therefore never become weary or dispirited, but in union with God's own elect, who call upon Him day and night, entreat Him and even weary Him by our incessant entreaties that the Holy Spirit may again assume His rightful place and exercise full dominion in ourselves and the Church as a whole: yea, more, that He may again have His true place in the Church, be held in honour by all, and in everything reveal the glory of our Lord Jesus. To the soul that in sincerity prays according to His Word, God's answer will surely come.

There is nothing so fitted to search and to cleanse the heart as true prayer. It teaches one to put him to himself such questions as these: Do I really desire what above everything I pray for? Am I willing to cast out everything to make room for what God is prepared to give me? Is the prayer of my lips really the prayer of my life? Do I really continue in inter-

[1] Acts xiii. 2, 3.

course with God, waiting upon Him, in quiet trust, until He gives me this great, heavenly, supernatural gift, *His own Spirit*, to be my spirit, the spirit of my life every hour?

O let us "pray always and not faint," setting ourselves before God with supplications and strong crying as His priests and the representatives of His Church. We may reckon upon it that He will hear us.

> "In my distress I called upon the Lord,
> And cried unto my God:
> He heard my voice out of His temple,
> And my cry before Him came into His ears.
> He delivered me from my strong enemy,
> He brought me forth also into a large place."[1]

Brother, you know that the Lord is a God that often hideth Himself. He desires to be trusted. He is oftentimes very near to us without our knowing it. He is a God who knows His own time. Yet, "though He tarry, wait for Him. He will surely come. He will not tarry."[2]

[1] Psa. xviii. 6, 17, 19 (R.V.).   [2] Hab. ii. 3.

CHAPTER I

HOW IT IS TO BE TAUGHT

"And it came to pass that Paul came to Ephesus and found certain disciples: and he said unto them, Did ye receive the Holy Spirit when ye believed?"—Acts xix. 1-2.

IT was about twenty years after the outpouring of the Holy Spirit that the incident which is referred to in the beginning of this chapter of the Acts took place. In the course of his journey Paul came to Ephesus, and found in the Christian church there some disciples in whom he observed that there was something lacking in their belief or experience. Accordingly he put to them the question: "Did ye receive the Holy Spirit when ye believed?" Their reply was that they had not yet heard of the Holy Spirit. They had been baptized by disciples of John the Baptist with the baptism of repentance with a view to faith in Jesus as One who was to come; but with the great event of the outpouring of the Spirit or the significance of it they were still unacquainted. They came from a region of the country into which the full Pentecostal preaching of the exalted Saviour had not yet penetrated. Accordingly, Paul took them at once under his care, made them conversant with the full gospel of the glorified Lord, who had received the Spirit from the Father and had sent Him down to this world, that every one of His believing disciples might also receive Him. Hearing this glad tidings and consenting to it, they were baptized into the name of this Saviour, who baptizes with the Holy Spirit. Thereupon Paul prayed for them and laid his hands upon them, and they received the Holy Spirit; and then, in token of the fact that this whole transaction was a heavenly reality, they obtained a share in the Pentecostal miracle, and spake "with other tongues."

In these chapters it is my desire to bring to the children of God the message that there is a twofold Christian life. The one is that in which we experience something of the operations of the Holy Spirit, just as many did under the old covenant, but do not yet receive Him as the Pentecostal Spirit, as the personal indwelling Guest, concerning whom we know that He has come to abide permanently in the heart. On the other hand, there is a more abundant life, in which the indwelling just referred to is known and the full joy and power of redemption are fact of personal experience. It will be only when Christians come to understand fully the distinction betwixt these two conditions, and discern that the second of these is in very deed the will of God concerning them, and therefore a possible experience for each believer; when with shame and confusion of face they shall confess the sinful and inconsistent elements that still mark their life; that we shall dare to hope that the Christian community will once more be restored to its Pentecostal power. It is with our eye fixed on this distinction that we desire to ponder the lessons presented to us in the record of this incident at Ephesus.

I

For a healthful Christian life, it is indispensable that we should be fully conscious that we have received the Holy Spirit to dwell in us.

Had it been otherwise, Paul would never have put the question: "Did ye receive the Holy Spirit when ye believed?" These disciples were recognized as believers. This position, however, was not enough for them. The disciples who walked with the Lord Jesus on earth were also true believers, yet He commanded them not to rest satisfied until they had received the Holy Spirit from Himself in heaven. Paul too had seen the Lord in His heavenly glory and was by that vision led to conversion; yet even in his case the spiritual work he required to have done in him was not thereby completed. Ananias had to go to him and lay his hands upon him that he might receive the Holy Spirit. Only then could he become a witness for Christ. All these facts teach us that there are two ways in which the Holy Spirit works in us. The first is the preparatory operation in which He simply acts on us but does not yet take up His abode within us, though leading us to conversion and faith and ever urging us to all that is good and holy. The second is the higher and more advanced phase of His working when we receive Him as an abiding gift, as an indwelling Person, concerning whom we know that He assumes responsibility for our whole inner being, working in it both to will and to do. This is the ideal of the full Christian life.

II

There are disciples of Christ who know little or nothing of this conscious indwelling of the Holy Spirit.

It is of the utmost importance to understand and hold fast this statement. The more fully we come under the conviction of its truth, the better shall we understand the condition of the Church in our times and be at last enabled to discover where we ourselves really stand.

The condition I refer to becomes very plain to us when we consider what took place at Samaria. Philip the evangelist had preached there; many had been led to believe in Jesus and were baptized into His name; and there was great joy in that city. When the apostles heard this news, they sent down Peter and John, who, when they came to Samaria, prayed that these new converts might receive the Holy Spirit.[1] This gift was thus something quite different from the working of the Spirit that led them to conversion and faith and joy in Jesus as a Saviour. It was something higher: for now from heaven, and by the glorified Lord Himself, the Holy Spirit was imparted in power with His abiding indwelling, to consecrate and fill their hearts.

If this new experience had not been bestowed, the Samaritan disciples would still indeed have been Christians, but they would have remained weak, defective, and sickly; and thus it is that in our own days there is still many a Christian life that knows nothing of this bestowment of the Holy Spirit. Amidst much that is good and amiable, with even much earnestness and zeal, the life of such Christians is still hampered by weakness and stumbling and disappointment, simply because it has never been brought into vitalising contact with power from on high, because such souls have not received the Holy Spirit as the Pentescostal gift, to be possessed, and kept, and filled by Him.

[1] Acts viii. 16, 17.

III

It is the great work of the gospel ministry to lead believers to the Holy Spirit.

Was it not the great aim of the Lord Jesus, after He had educated and trained His disciples for three years by His intercourse with them, to lead them up to the point of waiting for the promise of the Father and receiving the Holy Spirit sent down from heaven? Was not this the chief object of Peter on the day of Pentecost, when, after summoning those who were pricked in their hearts to repent and be baptized for the forgiveness of sins, he assured them that they should then receive the Holy Spirit?[1] Was it not this also that Paul aimed at when in his Epistles he asked his fellow-Christians if they did not know that they were each one "a temple of the Holy Spirit," or reminded them that they had to be "filled with the Holy Spirit"?[2] Yes: the supreme need of the Christian life is to receive the Holy Spirit, and when we have it, to be conscious of the fact and live in harmony with it. An evangelical minister must not merely preach about the Holy Spirit from time to time or even often-times, but also direct all his efforts towards teaching his congregation that there can be no true worship save through the indwelling and unceasing operation of the Holy Spirit.

IV

To lead believers to the Holy Spirit, the great lack in their life must be pointed out to them.

This was manifestly the intention in Paul's question: "Did ye receive the Holy Spirit when ye believed?" Just as

[1] Acts ii. 38. [2] Cor. vi. 19; Eph. v. 18.

only those that are thirsty will drink water with eagerness and only those that are sick will desire a physician, so it is only when believers are prepared to acknowledge the defective and sinful character of their spiritual condition, that the preaching of the full blessing of Pentecost will find an entrance into their hearts. So long as Christians imagine that the only thing lacking in their life is more earnestness, or more importunity, or more strength, and that if they only obtain these benefits they themselves will become all they ought to be, the preaching of a full salvation will be of little avail. It is only when the discovery is made that they are not standing in a right attitude towards the Holy Spirit, that they have only His preparatory operations, but do not yet know and honour Him in His indwelling, that the way to something higher will ever be open or even be desired. For this discovery, it is indispensable that the question should be put to each, man by man, as pointedly and as personally as may be: "Did ye receive the Holy Spirit when ye believed?" When the answer shall take the shape of a deeply felt and utterly sincere Alas! the time of revival is not far off.

V

Believers must receive help to appropriate this blessing in faith.

In the Acts of the Apostles we read often about laying on of hands and prayer. Even a man like Paul—whose conversion was due to the direct interposition of the Lord, and was therefore so effectual—had to receive the Spirit through laying on of hands and prayer on the part of

Ananias.[1] This implies that there must be amongst ministers of the gospel and believers generally a power of the Spirit which makes them the channel of faith and courage to others. Those who are weak must be helped to appropriate the blessing for themselves. But those who have and bring this blessing, as well as those who desire to have it, must realize and acknowledge their absolute dependence on the Lord and expect all from Him.

The gift of the Spirit is imparted only by God Himself. Every fresh bestowment of the Spirit comes from above. There must be frequent personal dealing with God. The minister of the Spirit whom God is to use for communicating the blessing as well as the believer who is to receive it, must meet with God in immediate and closest intercourse. Every good gift comes from above: it is faith in this truth that will give us courage to expect with confidence and gladness that the full Pentecostal blessing may confidently be looked for, and that a life under the continual leading of the Holy Spirit is within our reach.

VI

The proclamation and appropriation of this blessing will restore the Christian community to the primary Pentecostal power.

On the day of Pentecost the speaking "with other tongues" and the prophesying was the result of being filled with the Spirit. Here at Ephesus, twenty years later, the very same miracle is again witnessed, as the visible token and pledge of the other glorious gifts of the Spirit. We may reckon upon it that where the reception of the

[1] Acts ix. 17.

Holy Spirit and the possibility of being filled with Him are proclaimed and appropriated, the blessed life of the Pentecostal community will be restored in all its pristine power.

In our days there is an increasing acknowledgment of the lack of power in the Church of the Lord. In spite of all the multiplication of the means of grace, there is neither the power of the divine salvation in believers, nor the power for conversion in preaching, nor the power in the conflict of the Church with wordliness and unbelief and unrighteousness that, according to God's Word, we are bound to look for. The complaint is made with justice. Would that the expression of it became so strong that the children of God, driven by a keen sense of need, might be led to cast themselves upon the great truth which the Word of God teaches—namely, that it is only when faith in the full Pentecostal blessing and the full enjoyment of it are found in the Christian Church that the members of it shall again find their strength and be able to do their first works.

VII

The most urgent need of the Church is that of men who shall be able to bear testimony to this blessing.

Whether it be of teachers like Peter and Paul, of deacons like Philip, or of ordinary believers like Ananias who came to Paul, this is our first need. It furnishes abundant reason why teachers and members of congregations should unitedly call upon God, that alike in preaching and pastoral intercourse there may be more manifest proof that those who preach Christ Jesus may preach Him as John the Baptist did, as the One who baptizes with the Holy Spirit. It is only the minister that stands forth as a personal witness and living proof of the ministry of the Spirit whose word will have full entrance into the hearts of the people and exercise full sway over them. The first disciples obtained the baptism on their knees; on their knees they obtained it for others. It will be on our knees also that the full blessing will be won to-day. On our knees: let this be the attitude in which we await the full blessing of our God, alike in our individual and collective life.

Have ye received the Holy Spirit since ye believed? Let every reader submit himself to this heart-searching question. To be filled with the Holy Spirit of God, to have the full enjoyment of the Pentecostal blessing, is the will of God concerning us. Let us judge our life and our work before the Lord in the light of this question, and return the answer to God. O do not be afraid, my brother, to confess before your Lord what is still lacking in you. Do not keep back, although you do not as yet fully understand what the blessing is or how it comes. The early disciples did not know that, yet they called upon their Lord and waited for it with prayer and supplications. Let but your heart be filled with a deep conviction of what you lack, a desire for what God offers, a willingness to sacrifice everything for it, and you may rest assured that the marvel of Jerusalem and of Samaria, of Cæsarea and Ephesus, will once again be repeated. We may, we shall, be filled with the Spirit. Amen.

CHAPTER II

HOW GLORIOUS IT IS

"They were all filled with the Holy Spirit."—Acts ii. 4.

WHENEVER we speak of being filled with the Holy Spirit, and desire to know what it precisely is, our thoughts always turn back to the day of Pentecost. There we see as in a mirror how glorious the blessing is that is brought from heaven by the Holy Spirit and with which He can fill the hearts of men.

There is one fact which makes the great event of the day of Pentecost doubly instructive—this, namely, that we have learned to know very intimately the men who were then filled with the Spirit, by their intercourse for three years with the Lord Jesus. Their infirmities and defects, their sins and perversities, all stand open to our view. But the blessing of Pentecost wrought a complete transformation. They became entirely new men, so that one might say of them with truth: "Old things have passed away: behold all is become new." Close study of them and their example helps us in more than one way. It shows us to what weak and sinful men the Spirit will come. It teaches us how they were prepared for the blessing. It teaches us also—and this is the principal thing— how mighty and complete the revolution is that is brought to pass when the Holy Spirit is received in His fulness.

It lets us see how glorious the grace that awaits us is if we press on to the full blessing of Pentecost.

I

The ever-abiding presence and indwelling of the Lord Jesus.

In this we have the first and principal blessing of the Pentecostal life. In the course of our Lord's intercourse with His disciples on earth He spared no pains to teach and train them, to renew and sanctify them. In most respects, however, they remained just what they were. The reason was that up to this point He was ever still nothing more than an external Christ who stood outside of them and from without sought to work upon them by His word and His personal influence. With the advent of Pentecost this condition was entirely changed. In the Holy Spirit He came down as the inward indwelling Christ, to become in the very innermost recesses of their being the life of their life. This is what He Himself had promised in the words: "I will not leave you orphans: *I come unto you*. In that day ye shall know that I am in My Father, and ye in Me, and I in you."[1] This was the source of all the other blessings that came with Pentecost. Jesus Christ, the Crucified, the Glorified, the Lord from heaven, came in spiritual power, by the Spirit, to impart to them that ever-abiding presence of their Lord that had been promised to them; and that indeed in a way that was at once most intimate, all-powerful, and wholly divine: by the indwelling which makes Him in truth their life. Him

[1] John xiv. 18, 20.

whom they had had in the flesh, living with them on earth, they now received by the Spirit in His heavenly glory within them. Instead of an outward Jesus near them, they now obtained the inward Jesus with them.

II

From this first and principal blessing sprang the second: *the Spirit of Jesus came into them as the life and the power of sanctification*.

Here I shall allude at the outset to only one feature in this change. We know how often the Lord had to rebuke them for their pride and exhort them to humility. It was all of no avail. Even on the last night of His earthly life, at the table of the Holy Supper, there was a strife amongst them as to which of them should be the greatest.[1] The outward teaching of the outward Christ, whatever other influences it may have exercised, was not sufficient to redeem them from the power of indwelling sin; this could be achieved only by the indwelling Christ. Only when Jesus descended into them by the Holy Spirit did they undergo a complete change. They received Him in His heavenly humility and subjection to the Father, and in His self-sacrifice for others, as their life. Henceforth all was changed. From that moment onwards they were animated by the spirit of the meek and lowly Jesus.

This, in very truth, is still the only way to a real sanctification, to a life that actually overcomes sin. It is just because so many preachers and so many Christians keep their minds occupied only with the external Christ on the Cross or in heaven, and wait for the blessing of

[1] Luke xxii. 24.

His teaching and His working without understanding that the blessing of Pentecost brings Him *into us*, to work Himself all *in us*, that they make so little progress in sanctification. Christ Himself is of God made unto us sanctification: and that in no other way than by our living and being moved and existing in Him, because He lives and abides in our heart and works all there.

III

An overflowing of the heart with the love of God is also a part of the blessing of Pentecost.

Next to pride, lack of love—or, as we may put it in one word, lovelessness—was the sin for which the Lord had so often to rebuke His disciples. These two sins have in truth one and the same root: the self-seeking *I*, the desire for self-pleasing. The new commandment that He gave them, the token whereby all men should know that they were His disciples, was love to one another. How gloriously was it manifested on the day of Pentecost that the Spirit of the Lord shed abroad His love in the hearts of His own. The multitude of them that believed were as one heart, one soul: all things they possessed were held in common; no one said that anything of that which he had was his own. The kingdom of heaven with its life of love had come down to them. The spirit, the disposition, the wonderful love of Jesus, filled them, because He Himself had come into them.

How closely the mighty working of the Spirit and the indwelling of the Lord Jesus are bound up with a life in love appears from the prayer of Paul in behalf of the Ephesians, in which he asks that they might be

strengthened with power *by the Spirit*, in order that
Christ might dwell in their hearts. Then he forthwith
makes this addition: "that ye, being rooted and grounded
in love, may be strong to apprehend the love which
passeth knowledge."[1] The filling with the Spirit and the
indwelling of Christ bring of themselves a life that has
its root, its joy, its power, its evidence in love, because the
indwelling Christ Himself is Love. O how would the
love of God fill the Church and convince the world that
she has received a heavenly element into her life, if the
filling with the Spirit and the indwelling of Christ in the
heart were recognized as the blessing which the Father
has promised us!

IV

*The coming of the Spirit changed weakness and fear
into courage and power.*

We all know how, from fear rising in his heart at the
word of a woman, Peter denied his Lord; and how that
same night all the disciples fled and forsook Him. Their
hearts were really attached to Him, and they were sincerely willing to do what they had promised and go to
die with Him; but when it came to the crisis, they had
neither courage nor power. They had to say: "To will
is present with me, but how to perform I find not." After
the blessing of the Spirit of Pentecost, there was no more
question of merely willing apart from performing. By
Christ dwelling in us God works both the willing and
the doing. With what confidence of spirit did Peter on
the day of Pentecost dare to preach the Crucified One to

[1] Eph. iii. 16-19.

thousands of hostile Jews. With what boldness was he able, in opposition to the leaders of the people, to say: "We must obey God rather than men."[1] With what courage and joy were Stephen and Paul and so many others enabled to encounter threatening and suffering and death: they did this even triumphantly. It was because the Spirit of Christ, the Victor,—yea, the Christ Himself, who had been glorified,—dwelt within them. It is the joy of the blessing of Pentecost that gives courage and power to speak for Jesus, because by it the whole heart is filled with Him.

V

The blessing of Pentecost makes the whole Word of God new.

How distinctly do we see this fact in the case of the disciples. As with all the Jews of that age, their ideas of the Messiah and the kingdom of God were utterly external and carnal. All the instruction of the Lord Jesus throughout three long years could not detach their minds from them. They were utterly unable to comprehend the doctrine of a suffering and dying Messiah or the hope of His invisible spiritual dominion. Even after His resurrection He had to rebuke them for their unbelieving spirit and their backwardness in understanding the Scriptures. With the coming of the day of Pentecost an entire change took place. The whole of their ancient Scriptures opened up before them. The light of the Holy Spirit in them illumined the Word. In the preaching of Peter and

[1] Acts v. 29.

Stephen, in the addresses of Paul and James, we see how a divine light had shone upon the word of the Old Testament. They saw everything through the Spirit of this Jesus who had made His abode within them.

So will it be also with ourselves. It is as necessary as it is helpful that we should study the Scriptures and meditate upon them, and keep the word of God alike in head and heart and daily walk. Let us, however, constantly remember that it is only when we are filled with the Spirit that we can rightly and fully experience the spiritual power and truth of the Word. He is "the Spirit of truth." He alone guides into all truth when He dwells in us.

VI

It is the blessing of Pentecost that gives power to bless others.

The divine power of the exalted Jesus to grant repentance and the forgiveness of sins is exercised by Him through His servants whom He sends forth to proclaim these blessings. The minister of the gospel who desires to preach repentance and forgiveness through Jesus with success in winning souls, must do the work in the power of the Spirit of this Jesus. The chief reason why so much preaching of conversion and pardon is fruitless lies in the fact that these elements of truth are presented only as a doctrine, and that preachers endeavour to secure a way to the hearts of their audience in the power of merely human earnestness, and reasoning, and eloquence. But little blessing is won by these means. It is the man that makes it his chief desire to be filled with the Spirit of

God, and then by faith in the indwelling of Christ comes
to be assured that the glorified Lord will speak and work
in him, who will obtain blessing. It is true, indeed, that
this blessing will not always be given in the very same
measure or in the very same manner, but it will always
certainly come: just because the preacher permits the Lord
to work in and through him. Alike in preaching and in
the daily life of a servant of Christ, the full blessing of
Pentecost is the sure way of becoming a blessing to others.
"He that believeth on Me," said Jesus, "out of his belly
shall flow rivers of living water."[1] This he said of the
Holy Spirit. A heart filled with the Spirit will overflow
with the Spirit.

VII

*It is the blessing of Pentecost that will make the Church
of Christ what God would have her be.*

We have spoken of what the Spirit will do in individual
believers. We have also to think of what the blessing
will be when the Church as a whole shall apprehend her
calling to be filled with the Spirit, and then to exhibit
the life and the power—yea, and the very presence—of
her Lord to the world. We must not only seek and receive
this blessing, every one for himself, but we must also
remember that the full manifestation of what the blessing
itself is, cannot be given until the whole body of Christ
be filled with it. "If one member suffer, all the members
suffer with it."[2] If many members of the Church of Christ
are content to remain without this blessing, the whole
Church will suffer. Even in individual disciples the bless-

[1] John vii. 38.   [2] Cor. xii. 26.

ing cannot come to its full manifestation. Hence it is of the utmost importance that we should not only think of what the being "filled with the Spirit" means for ourselves, but also consider what it will do for the Church, especially in our own neighbourhood, and by her for all the world.

To this end, let us simply recall the morning of the day of Pentecost. At that juncture the Christian Church in Jerusalem consisted only of one hundred and twenty disciples, most of them poor unlearned fishermen, publicans, and humble women, an insignificant and despised gathering.[1] Yet it was just by these believers that the kingdom of God had to be proclaimed and extended: and they did it. By them, and those who were added to them, the power of Jewish prejudice and of pagan hardness of heart was overcome, and the Church of Christ won glorious triumphs. This grand result was achieved simply and only because the first Christian Church was filled with the Spirit. The members of it gave themselves wholly to their Lord. They allowed themselves to be filled and consecrated, governed and used only by Him. They yielded themselves to Him as instruments of His power. He dwelt in them and wrought in them all His wondrous deeds.

It is to this same experience that the Church of Christ in our age must be brought back. This is the only thing that will help her in the conflict with mere civilization or paganism, with sin or the world. She must be filled with the Spirit.

Beloved fellow-Christians, this summons comes to you. "One thing is needful." Alike for yourselves and the whole Church of the Lord, this is the one thing that is

[1] Acts i. 15.

needful: we have to be filled with the Spirit. Pray do
not imagine that you must comprehend or understand
it all before you seek and find it. For those that wait
upon Him God will do even that which has not yet
entered into their heart to conceive. If you would taste
the happiness, if you would know by personal experience
the unutterable blessedness, of having Jesus in the heart,
of having in you His Spirit of holiness and humility, of
love and self-sacrifice, of courage and power, as naturally
and continuously as you have your own spirit; if you
would have the Word of God in you as light and power,
and be enabled to carry it about as a blessing for others,
if you would fain see the Church of Christ stand forth
arrayed in her first splendour—then separate yourselves
from everything that is evil, cast it utterly out of your
heart, and fix your desire on this one thing: to be filled
with the Spirit of God. Reckon upon receiving this as your
rightful heritage. Appropriate it and hold it fast by faith.
It shall certainly be given to you.

CHAPTER III

HOW IT WAS BESTOWED FROM HEAVEN

"If ye love Me, ye will keep My commandments. And I will pray the Father, and He shall give you another Comforter, that He may be with you for ever, even the Spirit of truth."—John xiv.

A TREE lives always according to the nature of the seed from which it sprang. Every living being is always guided and governed by the nature which it received at its birth. Thus the Church of Christ received the promise and the law of her existence and her growth in that which was bestowed upon her in the Holy Spirit on the day of her birth. This is the reason why it is of such importance for us to turn back often to the day of Pentecost and not to rest until we thoroughly understand, and receive, and experience what God did for His people on that day. When we see how the blessing was then for the first time given from heaven, and what the disposition of heart was that fitted the disciples for receiving the Spirit, then we know for all coming time what remains to be done by ourselves to enjoy the same blessing. The first disciples serve us as examples and forerunners on the way to the fulness of the Spirit.

What, then, was there in them which enabled them to become the recipients of these heavenly gifts and made

them fit objects of the unspeakable grace that in them
first of all the Three-One God came to take up His abode?
The right answer to this question will help us not a little
on the way to be filled with the Holy Spirit.

What do we find in these first disciples?

I

In the first place, there is the fact that *they were deeply
attached to the Lord Jesus.*

The Son of God came into the world in order to unite
the divine life which He had with the Father with the life
of man, and thus to secure that the life of God should
penetrate into the life of the creature. When He had
completed the work in His own person by His obedience,
and death, and resurrection, He was exalted to the throne
of God on high in order that in spiritual power, and not
only apart from the limitations of earthly life but in the
might of the all-penetrating sovereign presence of God,
His disciples and His Church might participate in His
own very life. We read that the Holy Spirit "was not yet,
because Jesus was not yet glorified."[1] It was only after His
glorification that the Holy Spirit, as the Spirit of Godhead
united with manhood, the Spirit of the complete indwelling of God in man, could be given. It is the Spirit
of the glorified Jesus that the disciples received on the day
of Pentecost, the Spirit of the Head, penetrating all the
members of His body.

It is evident without proof that, if the fulness of the
Spirit thus dwells in Jesus, *a personal relationship to Him*

[1] John vii. 39.

is the first condition for the reception of the full gift of the Comforter. It was to attain this end that the Lord Jesus throughout all His three years' work on earth kept the disciples in such close converse with Himself. He desired to attach them to Himself. He wanted them to feel themselves truly one with Him. He wanted them to identify themselves with Him, as far as this was possible. By knowledge and intercourse, by love and obedience, they became inwardly knit to Him. This was the preparation for participating in the Spirit of His glorification.

The lesson that is here taught us is indeed extremely simple, but it is one of profound significance. There are not a few Christians who believe in the Lord and are very zealous in His service, who eagerly desire to become holy, and who yet do not succeed in their endeavour. It seems oftentimes as if they could not understand the promise of the Spirit. The thought of being filled with the Spirit exercises but little influence upon them. The reason is obvious. There is lacking in their religion that personal relationship to the Lord Jesus, that inward attachment to Him, that perfectly natural reference to Him as the best and nearest Friend, as the beloved Lord, which was so characteristic of the disciples. This, however, is absolutely indispensable. It is a heart that is entirely occupied with the Lord Jesus, and depends only upon Him, that can alone hope for the fulness of the Spirit.

II

They had left all for Jesus.

"Nothing for nothing." This proverb contains a deep

truth. A thing that costs me nothing may nevertheless cost me much. It may bring me under an obligation to the giver, and so cost me more than it is worth. I may have so much trouble in appropriating it and keeping it that I may pay much more for it than the price which should be asked for it. "Nothing for nothing": the maxim holds good also in the life of the kingdom of heaven. The parables of the Pearl of great price and the Treasure hid in a field teach us that, in order to obtain possession of the kingdom within us, we must sell all that we have. This is the very renunciation that Jesus literally demanded of the disciples who had to follow Him. This is the requirement He so often repeated in His preaching: "He that forsaketh not all that he hath cannot be My disciple."[1] The two worlds betwixt which we stand are in such direct conflict with one another, and the world in which we by nature live exercises such a mighty influence over us, that it is often necessary for us, even by external and visible sacrifice, to withdraw from it. It was thus that Jesus trained His disciples to long for that which is heavenly. Only thus could He prepare them to desire and receive the heavenly gift with an undivided heart.

The Lord has left us no outward directions as to how much of the world we are to abandon or in what manner. But by His whole Word He teaches us that without sacrifice, without a deliberate separation from the world and forsaking of it, we shall never make much progress in grace. The spirit of this world has penetrated so deeply into us that we do not observe it. We share in its desire for comfort and enjoyment, for self-pleasing and self-

[1] Luke xiv. 33.

exaltation, without our knowing how impossible these things make it for us to be filled with the Spirit. Let us learn from the early disciples that to be filled from the heavenly world with the Spirit that dwells there, we must be entirely separate from the children of this world or from worldly Christians. We must be ready and eager to live as entirely different men, who literally represent heaven upon earth, because we have received the Spirit of the King of Heaven.

III

Thy had despaired utterly of themselves and all that is of man.

Man has two great enemies by whom the devil tempts him and with whom he has to contend. The one is the world without, the other is the self-life within. This last, the selfish *Ego,* is much more dangerous and stronger than the first. It is quite possible for a man to have made much progress in forsaking the world while the self-life retains ful dominion within him. You see this fact illustrated in the case of the disciples. Peter could say with truth: "Lo! we have left all and followed Thee." Yet how manifestly did the selfish *Ego,* with its self-pleasing and its self-confidence, still retain its full sway over him.

As the Lord at their first calling led them up to the point of forsaking their outward possessions and following Him, so shortly afterwards He began to teach them that a disciple must deny himself and lose his own life if he would be worthy of receiving His. He must hate not only father and mother, where this was necessary, but even his

own life. It was love for this self-life, more than all love
for father and mother, that hindered the Lord Jesus from
doing His work in the heart. It was to cost them more
to be redeemed from the selfish *Ego* within them than to
get quit of the world around them. The self-life is the
natural life of sinful man. He can be liberated from it
by nothing save by death—that is, by first dying to it and
then living in the strength of the new life that comes
from God.

The forsaking of the world began at the outset of the
three years' discipleship. It was at the end of that period,
at the Cross of Jesus, that dying to the self-life first took
place. When they saw Him die, they learned to despair
of themselves and of everything on which they had
hitherto based their hope. Whether they thought of their
Lord and the redemption which they had expected, or
whether they thought of themselves and their shameful
unfaithfulness towards Him, everything tended to fill
them with despair. Little did they know that it was just
this despair which was to prove the breaking up of their
hard hearts—the mortification of the self-life and of
confidence in themselves—which would enable them to
receive something entirely new—namely, a divine life
through the Spirit of the glorified Jesus in the innermost
depths of their souls.

O that we understood better that there is nothing which
so hampers us as secret reliance on something in ourselves
or in the Church around us, which we imagine can help
us! On the other hand, there is nothing that brings so
much blessing as entire despair of ourselves and of all
that is upon the earth, in the way of teaching us to turn

our hearts only and wholly to heaven and to partake of
the heavenly gift which comes thence.

IV

*They received and held fast the promise of the Spirit
given by the Lord Jesus.*

We know how, in His farewell address on the last
night of His sojourn on earth, Jesus comforted His
disciples in their sorrow over His departure with one
great promise—namely, the mission of the Holy Spirit
from heaven. This was to be better than His own bodily
presence among them. It would be to them the full fruit
and power of His redemption. The divine Life—yea, He
Himself, with the Father—was to make abode within
them. The unheard-of wonder, the mystery of the ages,
was to be their portion. They were to know that they were
in Him and He in them. At His ascension from the Mount
of Olives, this promise of the Spirit was the subject of
the last words He addressed to them.

It is evident that the disciples had still but little idea of
what this promise signified. But however defective their
understanding of it was, they held it fast; or rather, the
promise held them fast and would not let them go. They
all had only one thought : something has been promised to
us by our Lord; it will give us a share in His heavenly
power and glory; we know for certain that it is coming.
Of what the thing itself was, or of what their experience
of it was to be, they could give no account. It was enough
for them that they had the word of the Lord. He would
make it a blessed reality within them.

Now it is just the same disposition which we have so much need of now. To us also, even as to them, has the word of the Lord come concerning the Spirit who is to descend from the throne in the power of his glorified life. "He that believeth in Me, out of his heart shall flow rivers of living water." For us also it is the one thing needful to hold fast that word; to set our whole desire upon the fulfilment of it; to lay aside all else, until we inherit the promise. The word from the mouth of Jesus concerning the reception of the Spirit in such measure that we shall be endued with power from on high must animate and fill us with strong desire, with firm and joyful assurance.

V

They waited upon the Father until the performance of the promise came and they were filled with the Spirit.

The ten days of waiting were for them days in which they were continually in the Temple "praising and blessing God" and "continuing instant in prayer and supplication." It is not enough for us to endeavour to strengthen desire and to hold fast our confidence. The principal thing is to set ourselves in close and abiding contact with God. The blessing must come from God; God Himself must give it to us; we are to receive the gift directly from Him. What is promised us is a wonderful work of divine Omnipotence and Love. What we desire is the personal occupancy and indwelling of God the Holy Spirit. God Himself must bestow this personally upon us. A man gives another a piece of bread or a piece of money. He gives it away from himself and has nothing further to do with it. It is not thus with God's gift of the Holy Spirit. No: the Spirit is God. God is in the Spirit who comes to us, even as He was in the Son. The gift of the Spirit is the most personal act of the Godhead: it is the gift of Himself unto us. We have to receive it in the very closest personal contact with God.

The clearer the insight we obtain into this principle, the more deeply shall we feel how little we can do to grasp the blessing by our own desiring, or endeavouring; or believing. No: all our desiring, and striving, and believing can only issue in a more complete acknowledgment that we ourselves can do nought to win the boon. It is the Goodness of God alone that must give it; it is His Omnipotence that must work it in us. Our disposition must be one of silent assurance that the Father desires to give it to us; that He will not keep us waiting one moment longer than is absolutely necessary; and that there shall not be a single soul which persists in waiting in the pathway of self-abnegation and dependence that shall not be filled with the glory of God.

Every tree continues always to grow from the root out of which it first sprang. The day of Pentecost was the planting of the Christian Church, and the Holy Spirit became the power of its life. Let us turn back to that experience. There is our power still. We learn from the disciples what is really necessary. Attachment to Jesus, the abandonment of everything in the world for Him, despair of self and of all help from man, holding on to the word of promise, and then waiting on God, "the living God"—this is the sure way of living in the joy and power of the Holy Spirit.

CHAPTER IV

HOW LITTLE IT IS ENJOYED

"My speech and my preaching were not in persuasive words of wisdom, but in demonstration of the Spirit and of power: that your faith should not stand in the wisdom of men, but in the power of God."—1 Cor. ii 4, 5.

PAUL speaks here of two kinds of preaching and two kinds of faith. According to the spirit of the preacher will be the faith of the congregation. When the preaching of the Cross is given only in the words of human wisdom, then the faith of the hearers will be in the wisdom of men. When the preaching is in demonstration of the Spirit and of power, the faith of the Christian people will also be in the power of God, at once firm and strong. Preaching in the demonstration of the Spirit will bring the double blessing of power in the word and power in the faith of those who receive that word. If we desire to know the measure of the working of the Spirit, we must consider the preaching and the faith that springs from it. In this way alone can we see whether the full blessing of Pentecost is truly manifested in the Church of Christ.

There are very few who are prepared to say that this is really the case. Everywhere among the children of God we hear complaints of weakness and sin. Amongst those who do not so complain, there is reason to fear that their silence is to be ascribed to the prevalence of ignorance or self-satisfaction. It is of the utmost import-ance that we should concentrate our thoughts upon this fact, until we come under the full conviction that the condition of the Church is marked by impotence, and that nothing can restore her but the return to a life in the full enjoyment of the blessing of Pentecost. The more deeply we feel our deficiency, the more speedily shall we desire and obtain restoration. It will help to awaken longing for this blessing, and to find out the way to obtain it, if we earnestly consider how little it is enjoyed in the Church and how far the Church is from being what her Lord has willingness and power to make her.

1

Think, for example, what little power over sin there is amongst the children of God.

The Spirit of Pentecost is the Holy Spirit, the Spirit of God's holiness. When He came down upon the desciples, what a transformation was effected in them. Their carnal thoughts were changed into spiritual insight, their pride into humility, their selfishness into love, their fear of man into courage and fidelity. Sin was cast out by the inflowing of the life of Jesus and of heaven.

The life which the Lord has prepared for His people is a life of victory. It is not indeed victory to such an extent as that there shall be no temptation to evil; nor yet that the inclination towards sin, inward sinfulness, shall be utterly rooted out of the flesh. But there is to be victory of such a kind that the indwelling power of the Spirit who fills us, the presence of the indwelling Saviour, shall keep sin in subjection, as the light subdues the darkness.

Yet, to what a small extent do we see power for victory over sin in the Church of Christ. On the contrary, how often, even amongst earnest Christians, do we see much untruthfulness and lack of honour, pride and self-esteem, selfishness and lack of love. How little are the traces of the image of Jesus—obedience, and humility, and love, and entire surrender to the will of God—seen even among the people of God. The truth is that we have become so accustomed to the confession of sin and unfaithfulness, of disobedience and backsliding, that it is no longer regarded as a matter for shame. We make the confession before each other, and then after the prayer rest comforted and content. O brethren, let us rather feel humbled and mourn over it! It is because so little of the full blessing of the Spirit is enjoyed or sought for that the children of God still commit so much sin, and have therefore so much to confess. Let every sin, whether in ourselves or others, serve as a summons to notice how much is lacking of the Spirit of God amongst us. Let every instance of failure in the fear of the Lord, in love, and holiness, and entire surrender to the will of God, only urge us the more unceasingly to call upon God to bring His Spirit once more to full dominion over the whole Church of Christ.

II

Think, too, how little there is of separation from the world.

When the Lord Jesus promised the Comforter, He said:

"Whom the world cannot receive." The spirit of this world, which is devotion to the visible, is in irreconcilable antagonism with the Spirit of Jesus in heaven, where God and His will are everything. The world has rejected the Lord Jesus; and, to whatever extent it may now usurp the Christian name, the world at heart is still the same untamable foe. It was for this reason that Jesus said of His disciples, and as indicating one of their chief distinctive marks: "They are not of the world, even as I am not of the world."[1] This, too, is the reason why Paul said: "We have received, not the spirit of this world, but the Spirit which is of God."[2] The two spirits, the spirit of the world and the Spirit of God, are engaged in a life-and-death conflict with one another.

Hence it is that God has always called upon His people to separate themselves from the world, and to live as pilgrims whose treasure and whose heart are in heaven. But is this what is really seen amongst Christians? Who shall dare to say so? When they have attained to a measure of unblamableness in walk and assurance of heaven, most Christians consider that they are at liberty to enjoy the world as fully as others. There is little to be seen of true heavenly-mindedness in conversation and walk, in disposition and endeavour. Is not this the case just because the fulness of the Spirit is so little enjoyed and sought for? Nothing but light can drive out darkness; and nothing but the Spirit of heaven can expel the spirit of the world. Where a man does not surrender himself to be filled with the Spirit of Jesus and the Spirit of heaven, there can be no other issue than that, Christian though he may be, he

[1] John xvii. 16   [2] I. Cor. ii 12.

must come under the power of the spirit of the world.
O listen to the piercing cry that rises from the whole
Church of Christ: "Who shall rescue us from the power
of this spirit of the world?" And let your answer be:
"Nothing, no one, save the Spirit of God. I must be filled
with the Spirit."

III

*Think how little there is of steadfastness and growth
in faith.*

There is nothing of which ministers, and especially
those who labour for the salvation of souls, have to complain more than that there are so many who for a time
are full of zeal and then fall away. We see, not only
among the young or in times of awakening, but even
among many that have for years maintained a good confession, that whenever they enter into another circle of
influence, and are put to the proof by prosperity or any
special form of temptation, they forthwith cease to
persevere. Whence does this unhappy result arise? From
nothing but the fact that the preaching is more with the
wisdom of persuasive words than in demonstration of the
Spirit and of power. Hence their faith also stands in the
wisdom and work of man rather than in the power of God.
So long as such people have the benefit of earnest and
instructive preaching, they continue to stand; whenever
they lose it, they begin to backslide. It is because the
current preaching is so little in the demonstration of the
Spirit that souls are brought so little into contact with the
living God. For the same reason, far too much of the

current faith is not in the power of God. Even the Word of God—which ought always only to be a guide pointing *towards God Himself*—becomes all too frequently a veil with the study of which the soul becomes occupied, and is thus kept back from meeting with God. The Word, and preaching, and means of grace become a hindrance in place of a help if they are not in demonstration of the Spirit. All external means of grace are things that inevitably change and fade. It is the Spirit alone that works a faith which stands in the power of God, and so remains strong and unwavering.

Whence comes it that there are so many who do not continue to stand? Let the answer of God to this question penetrate deeply into our hearts. There is a grave lack of the demonstration of the Spirit. Let every sad discovery of congregations, or of smaller circles, or of individuals that do not remain steadfast, or that do not grow in grace, serve as a summons to us to acknowledge that the full blessing of Pentecost is lost. This is what we long for and must have from God. Let all that is within us begin to thirst and cry out: "Come from the four winds, O thou Spirit of God, and breathe upon these dead souls, that they may live."

IV

Think how little there is of power for service amongst the unconverted.

What an immense host of workers there is in Christian countries. How varied and unceasing is the preaching of the Word. Sunday-school teachers are to be numbered by hundreds of thousands. How great is the number of Christian parents that make their children acquainted with the Word of God and would fain also bring them to the Lord as a Saviour. Yet how widespread is the acknowledgment of the little fruit that springs from all this work. How many there are who, notwithstanding all they hear, and in spite of the fact that they are by no means indifferent, are yet never laid hold of with power and helped to make a definite choice of salvation. How many also there are who from youth to old age are conversant with the Word of God but are never seized by it in the depths of their heart. They find it good, and pleasing, and instructive to attend church, but they have never felt the power of the Word as a hammer, and a sword, and a fire. The reason why they are so little disturbed is that the preaching they listen to is so little in demonstration of the Spirit and of power. Alas! there is evidence enough that there is but too great lack of the full blessing of Pentecost.

Does the blame for this issue attach to preachers or to congregations? My belief is that it belongs to both together. The preachers are the offspring of the Christian community. By the children we are enabled to see whether the mother is healthy or not. Preachers are very dependent on the life that is in their congregations. When a congregation finds satisfaction in the merely acceptable and instructive preaching of a young minister, it encourages him to go forward on the same path, whilst he should rather be helped by its elder or more advanced believers to seek earnestly the demonstration of the Spirit. When a minister does not lead his congregation, either in public worship or in private prayer, really to expect everything from the Spirit of God, then he is tempted, both for himself and his people, to put confidence in the wisdom of man and the work of man. O that we could lay it to heart, that, in the midst of all our lamentation over increasing worldliness of spirit and widespread indifference, the great cause of all impenitence is the lack of the full blessing of Pentecost! This alone gives power from on high which can break down and quicken again the hard hearts of men.

V

Think how little preparedness there is for self-sacrifice in behalf of the extension of the kingdom of God.

When the Lord Jesus at His ascension promised the Holy Spirit, it was as a power in us to work for Him. "Ye shall receive power, when the Holy Spirit is come upon you, and ye shall be My witnesses unto the uttermost parts of the earth."[1] The aim of the Pentecostal blessing from the King in heaven was simply to complete the equipment of His servants for His work as King upon the earth. No sooner did the Spirit descend upon them than they began to witness for Him. The Spirit filled them with the desire and the impulse, with the courage and the power, to brave all hostility and danger, to endure all suffering and persecution, if only they could succeed in making Jesus known as a Saviour. The Spirit of Pentecost was that true missionary Spirit which seeks to win the whole world for Jesus Christ.

It is often said in our days that the missionary spirit

---

[1] Acts i. 8.

is so much on the increase. Yet when we reflect carefully how little effort is expended on the missionary enterprise in comparison with what we bestow on our own interests, we shall see at once how feebly this question is still kindled in our hearts: "What more can I still sacrifice for Jesus? He offered Himself for me. I will offer myself wholly for Him and His work." It has been well said that the Lord measures our gifts not according to what we give, but according to what we retain. He who stands beside the treasury and observes what is cast into it still finds many who, like the widow, cast in all their living. But, alas! how many are there who with their five shillings or their five pounds have given only what they could never miss and what costs them little or no sacrifice. How far different would it be if the full blessing of Pentecost began to flow in. How would the hearts of men burn with love to Jesus, and out of very joy be impelled to give everything that He might be known as a Saviour all around, and that all might know His love.

Brother, contemplate the condition of the Church on earth, of the Christian community around you, of your own heart, and then say if there is not grave reason for the cry: "The full blessing of Pentecost: how little is it known." Ponder the present lack of sanctification, of separation from the world, of steadfastness amongst professing Christians, of conversions amongst the unsaved, and of self-sacrifice for the kingdom of God, and let the sad reality deepen in your soul the conviction that the Church is at present suffering from one great evil, and that this is her lack of the blessing of Pentecost. There can be no healing of her breaches, no restoration from her

fall, no renewing of her power, except by this one remedy
—namely, her being filled with the Spirit of God.

Let us then never cease to speak, think, mourn, and
pray over this trouble until this "one thing needful"
becomes the one thing that occupies our hearts. The
restoration is not easy. It will perhaps not come all at
once: it may not come speedily. The disciples of Jesus
required every day with Jesus for three long years to prepare them for it. Let us not be unduly discouraged if
the transformation we long for does not take place immediately. Let us feel the need and lay it to heart. Let
us continue instant in prayer. Let us stand fast in faith.
The blessing of Pentecost is the birthright of the Church,
the pledge of our inheritance, something that belongs to
us here on earth. Faith can never be put to shame. Cleav-
ing to Jesus with purpose of heart can never be in vain.
The hour will surely come when, if we believe persever-
ingly in Him, out of our hearts too will flow rivers of
living water. Amen.

CHAPTER V

HOW THE BLESSING IS HINDERED

"Then said Jesus unto His disciples: if any man would come after Me, let him deny himself, and take up his cross, and follow Me. For whosover would save his life shall lose it: and whosover shall lose his life for My sake shall find it."—Matt. xvi. 24, 25.

THERE are many who seek the full blessing of Pentecost long and earnestly and yet do not find it. Often the question is put as to what may be the cause of this failure. To this inquiry more than one answer may be given. Sometimes the solution of the problem points in the direction of one or another sin which is still permitted. Worldliness, lovelessness, lack of humility, ignorance of the secret of walking in the way of faith—these, and indeed many more causes, may also be often mentioned with justice. There are, however, many people who think that they have come to the Lord with what of these sources of failure still remains in them, and have sincerely confessed them and put them away, and yet complain that the blessing does not come. For all such it is particularly necessary to point out that there remains still one great hindrance—namely, the root from which all other hindrance have their beginning. This root is nothing else than our individual self, the hidden life of Self with its varied forms of self-seeking, self-pleasing, self-confidence, and self-satisfaction. The more earnestly anyone strives to obtain the blessing and would fain know what prevents him, the more certainly will he be led to the discovery that it is here the great evil lies. He himself is his worst foe: he must be liberated from himself; the self-life to which he clings must be utterly lost. Only then can the life of God entirely fill him.

That is what is taught us in the words of the Lord Jesus to Peter. Peter had uttered such a glorious confession of his Lord, that Jesus said to him: "Blessed art thou, Simon Bar-Jonah: for flesh and blood hath not revealed it unto thee, but My Father which is in heaven." But when the Lord began to speak of His death by crucifixion, the self-same Peter was seduced by Satan to say: "Be it far from Thee, Lord: this shall never be unto Thee."[1] Thereupon the Lord said to him that not only must He Himself lay down His life, but that this same sacrifice was to be made by every disciple. Every disciple must deny himself and take up his cross in order that he himself may be crucified and put to death on it. He that would fain save his life will lose it; and he that is prepared to lose his life for Christ's sake will find it.

You see, then, what the Lord here teaches and requires. Peter had learned through the Father to know Christ as the Son of God, but he did not yet know Him as the Crucified One. Of the absolute necessity of the Cross, and death on the Cross, he as yet knew nothing. It may be so with the Christian. He knows the Lord Jesus as his Saviour; he desires to know him better, yea, fully;

[1] Matt. xvi. 17, 22.

but he does not yet understand that for this end it is
necessary that he must have a deeper discernment of the
death of the Cross as a death which he himself must die;
that he must actually deny, and hate, and lose his life—
his whole life and being in the world—ere he can receive
the full life of God.

This requirement is hard and difficult. And why is this
so? Why should a Christian be called upon always to
deny himself, his own feeling, and will, and pleasure?
Why must he part with his life—that life to maintain
which a man is prepared to make any sacrifice? Why
should a man hate and lose his life? The answer is very
simple. It is because that life is so completely under the
power of sin and death that it has to be utterly denied
and sacrificed. The self-life must be wholly taken away
to make room for the life of God. He that would have
the full, the overflowing life of God, must utterly deny and
lose his own life.

You see it now, do you not? There is only one great
stumbling-block in the way of the full blessing of Pentecost. It lies in the fact that two diverse things cannot at
one and the same time occupy the very same place. Your
own life and the life of God cannot fill the heart at the
same time. Your life hinders the entrance of the life of
God. When your own life is cast out, the life of God
will fill you. So long as I *myself* am still something,
Jesus Himself cannot be everything. My life must be
expelled; then the Spirit of Jesus will flow in. Let every
seeker of the full blessing of Pentecost accept this principle and hold it fast. The subject is of such importance
that I should like to make it still clearer by pointing out

the chief lessons which these words of the Lord Jesus
teach us.

I

*Our life, our individual self, is entirely and completely
under the power of sin.*

When God created the angels and man, He gave them
a separate personality, a power over themselves, with the
intention that they should of their own free will present
and offer up that life, that individual self, to Him, in
order that He in turn might fill them with His life and
His glory. This was to be the highest blessedness of the
creature. It was to be a vessel filled with the life and the
perfection of God. The whole Fall alike of angels and of
men consisted of nothing but the perversion of their life,
their will, their personality, away from God, in order to
please *themselves.* This self-exaltation was the pride that
changed the angels into demons and cast them out of
heaven into hell. This pride was the infernal poison that
the serpent breathed into the ear and the heart of Eve.
Man turned himself away from God to find delight in
himself and the world. His life, his whole individuality,
was perverted and withdrawn from the control of God
that he might seek and serve *himself.* It was no wonder
that Jesus said: "You must hate, you must utterly lose
that life, ere the full life of the Spirit of God can be
yours. To the minutest details, always and in everything,
you must deny that self-life! otherwise the life of God
cannot possibly fill you. He that will come after Me, let
him deny *himself,* and take up his cross, and follow ME."[1]

[1] Matt. xvi. 24.

A deep conviction of the entire corruption of our nature, manifesting itself in the fact that even the Christian still pleases himself in many things, is an experience that is still lacking in many people. It appears to them both strange and harsh, when we say that in nothing is the Christian free to follow his own feeling, that self-denial is a requirement that must prevail in every sphere of life and without any exceptions. The Lord has never withdrawn His words: "He that forsaketh not all that he hath cannot be My disciple, cannot walk with Me, cannot be as I."[1]

II

Our own life must be utterly cast aside to make full room for the life of God.

At the time of his conversion the young Christian has but little understanding of this requirement. He receives the seed of the new life into his heart while the natural life is still strong. It was still thus with Peter when the Lord addressed to him the words that have been quoted. He was a disciple, but alas! how defective and incomplete. When his Lord was to die, instead of denying himself, he denied his Lord. But that grievous failure brought him at last to that despair of himself which caused him to go out and weep bitterly, and so prepared him for losing entirely his own life and for being wholly filled with the life of Jesus.

This, accordingly, is the point to which we must all in the long run come. So long as a Christian imagines that

[1] Luke xiv. 33.

in some things—for example, in his eating and drinking, in the spending of his time or money, in his thinking and speaking about others—he has still the right and the liberty to follow his own wishes, to please himself, to maintain his own life, he cannot possibly attain to the full blessing of Pentecost.

My brethren, it is an unspeakably holy and glorious thing that a man can be filled with the Spirit of God. It demands inevitably that the present occupant and governor of the heart, our individual self, shall himself be cast out, and that everything within it, everything wholly and entirely, shall be surrendered into the hands of the new Inhabitant, the Spirit of God. Would that we could understand that the joy and power of being filled with the Spirit will come of themselves when once we comply with the first and principal condition—namely, that He alone shall be acknowledged as our Life and our Leader.

III

It is once for all impossible for the Christian to bring about this great transformation in himself.

At no stage of our spiritual career are the power and the deceitfulness of our individual self and the self-life more manifest than in the attempt to grasp the full blessing of Pentecost. Many people endeavour to appropriate this blessing, and that by a great variety of efforts. They do not succeed, and they are not able to discover the reason why. They forget that Self-will can never cast out Self-will: that Self can never really mortify itself. Happy is the man who is brought up to the point of acknowledging his helplessness and impotence. He will here specially need to deny himself, and so cease to expect anything from his own life and strength, but will rather lay himself down in the presence of the Lord as one who is impotent and dead, that he may really receive the blessing from Him.

It was not Peter that prepared himself for the day of Pentecost or brought down the Pentecostal blessing from heaven; it was his Lord that did all this for him. His part was to despair of himself and yield himself to his Lord to accomplish in him what He had promised. Hence also it is your part, believer, while yielding obedience to this call, to deny *yourself*, and to lose *your own life*, and in presence of the Lord to sink down in your nothingness and impotence. Accustom yourself to set your heart before Him in deep humility, and silent patience, and childlike submission. The humility that is prepared to be nothing, the patience that will wait for Him and His time, the submission that will yield itself wholly that He may do what seemeth Him good, is all that you can do to show that you are ready to lose your life. Jesus, summons you to follow Him. Remember how He first sacrificed His will, and when He had laid down His life into the hands of the Father, and went down into the grave, waited till God raised Him again to life. Be you in like manner ready to lay down your life in weakness, and be assured that God will raise it up again in power with the fulness of the Spirit. Have done with the strength of mere personal efforts; abandon the dominion of your own power of apprehension. "Not by might, nor by power, but by My Spirit, saith the Lord."[1]

[1] Zech. iv. 6.

IV

It is the surrender of faith to Jesus in His self-humiliation and death that opens the way to the full blessing of Pentecost.

You of course say at once: "Who is sufficient for these things? Who can sacrifice everything and die and lay down his life utterly as Jesus did? To man such a surrender is impossible." My reply is that it is indeed so. But *"with God* all things are possible." You cannot literally follow Jesus, and like Him go down into death and the grave. That ever remains beyond your power. Never will our individual self yield itself up to death or rest quietly in the grave. But hear the glad tidings. In Christ you have died and have been buried. The power of His dying of His willing surrender of His spirit into the hands of the Father, of His silent resting in the grave, *works in you.* In faith in this working, however little you may understand it—in faith in this working in you of the spirit and the power of the death and the life of the Lord Jesus, give up yourself willingly to lose your life.

For this end, begin to regard the denying of yourself as the first and most necessary work of every day. Accept the message I bring you. The great hindrance in the way of the life of Pentecost is the self-life. Believe in the sinfulness, the detestableness, of that life: not on account of its gross external sins, but because it sets itself in the place of God; seeks, and pleases, and honours itself more than God. Exercise yourself in what Jesus lays upon you, and hate your own life as your own worst foe and as the foe of God. Begin to see what the full blessing is that

Jesus has prepared for you and which He bestowed at Pentecost—namely, His own life, His own indwelling; and count nothing too precious or too costly to give as an exchange for this pearl of great price.

Brother, are you really in earnest about having the full blessing of Pentecost and being filled with the Spirit of God? Is it your great desire to be made to know what hinders you from obtaining it? Take the word of our Lord and keep it in your heart. Take it and go with it to Himself. He is able to make you understand, and consider, and experience it. It is He who baptizes with the Holy Spirit. Let everything in you that belongs to self be sacrificed to Him, and be counted as loss, and cast away to give place to Himself. He who by His death obtained the Spirit, who prepared Peter for Pentecost in the fellowship of His suffering, has your guidance in His hands. Trust, O trust Him, your own Jesus. He baptizes with the Spirit, beyond doubt or question: deny yourself and follow Him; lose your own life and find His. Let Him impart Himself in the place you have hitherto retained for yourself. From Him there will flow rivers of living water. Amen.

CHAPTER VI

HOW IT IS OBTAINED BY US

"Be not drunken with wine, wherein is riot, but be filled with the Spirit."—Eph. v. 18.

THE command to be filled with the Spirit is just as peremptory as the prohibition not to be drunken with wine. As truly as we are not at liberty to be guilty of the vice are we bound not to be disobedient to the positive injunction. The same God who calls upon us to live in sobriety urges us with equal earnestness to be filled with the Spirit. His command is tantamount to a promise: a sure pledge that He Himself will give what He would fain see us possess. With full confidence in this fact, let us in all simplicity ask for the way in which in this respect we should live in the will of God, as those who would be filled with the Spirit. I desire now to suggest to those who really long for this blessing some directions whereby they may obtain what is prepared for them.

I

The full blessing of Pentecost is the inheritance of all the children of God.

This is the first principle we have to enunciate. There are many of God's children who do not fully believe this.

They imagine that the day of Pentecost was only the birth-day feast of the Church, and that it was thus a time of blessing and of power which was not destined to endure. They do not reflect on the command to be filled with the Spirit. The result is that they never with earnestness seek to receive the full blessing. They take their ease and remain content with the weak and defective life in which the Church of the day exists.

Is not this the case with you, my reader? Far be it from us. In order to carry on her work in the world, the Church requires the full blessing. To please your Lord and to live a life of holiness and joy, and power, you too have need of it. To manifest His presence, and indwelling, and glory in you, Jesus counts it necessary that you should be filled with the Spirit. Believe firmly that the full blessing of Pentecost is a sacred reality. A child of God may and must have it. Take time to contemplate it and to suffer yourself to be fully possessed by the thought of its glorious signi-ficance and power. A firm confidence that the blessing is actually within our reach is the first step towards obtaining it and a powerful impulse in the pursuit.

II

I do not as yet have this blessing.

This is the second step towards it. You may perhaps put the question why it should be necessary to cherish this conviction. I will tell you briefly the reasons why I consider it of importance.

The first is that there are many Christians who think

that they already have the Holy Spirit, and that all they require is to be more faithful in the endeavour to know and to obey Him. They think that they are already standing in God's grace, and that they only need to make a better use of the life they possess. They imagine that they have all that is necessary for continued growth. On the contrary, it is my deep conviction that such souls are in a sickly state and that they have need of a healing as divine and effective as that which the blind and lame received from the Lord on earth. Accordingly, just as the first condition of my recovery from disease is the knowledge that I am sick, so it is absolutely necessary for them to discover and acknowledge that they do not live the life of Pentecost, that they do not walk in the fulness and the joy of the Spirit, that they do not possess the full blessing which is indispensable for them if they are to please God in everything.

Once this first conviction is made thoroughly clear to them, they will be prepared for another consideration—namely, that they ought to acknowledge the guiltiness of their condition. They ought to see that if they have not yet rendered obedience to the command to "be filled with the Spirit," this defect is to be ascribed to sluggishness, and self-satisfaction and unbelief. They should be induced to acknowledge with shame that they have despised what God had prepared for them. When once the confession that they have not yet received the full blessing is deeply rooted in them, there will spring from it a stronger impulse to attain to it. Take, then, this thought and let it work in you with power: "No: it is true that I do not as yet have the full blessing."

III

The thought that will come next in succession is: *This blessing is for me.*

I have spoken of those who suppose that the full blessing of Pentecost was only for the first Christian community. There are others who are willing enough to acknowledge that it was intended also for the Church of later times but still think that all are not entitled to expect it. Eminent believers, the leaders of the Church, and such as have much leisure and abundant opportunity to occupy their minds with such attainments, may well cherish the hope of receiving this blessing, but it is not to be expected by ordinary members of the churches. Any one of these might quite reasonably say: "My unfavourable circumstances, my unfortunate disposition, my lack of real ability, and similar difficulties, make it impossible for me to realize this ideal. God will not expect this at my hands: He has not destined me to obtain it."

O soul, do not permit yourself to be deceived by such shallow views. All the members of a body, even to the very least, must be healthy before the body as a whole can be healthy. The indwelling, the fulness of the Spirit, is nothing but the entire healthfulness of the body of Christ. Be assured that, even though you are actually the most insignificant member of it, the blessing is for you. In your own little measure you can at least be full. In this respect the Father makes no exceptions. A great distinction doubtless prevails in point of gifts, and calling, and circumstances; but there can be no distinction in the love of the Father and his desire to see every one of His

children in full health and in the full enjoyment of the
Spirit of adoption. Learn, then, to express and to repeat
over again the conviction: "*This blessing is for me*. My
Father desires to have me that He may fill me with His
Spirit. The blessing lies before me, to be taken with my
full consent. I will no longer despise by unbelief what
falls to me as my birthright. With my whole heart I will
say: 'This blessing is for me'."

IV

I cannot grasp this blessing in my own power.

Whenever a Christian begins to strive for this blessing,
he generally makes a variety of efforts to reach after the
faith, and obedience, and humility, and submission which
are the conditions of obtaining it. Then, when he does not
succeed, he is tempted to blame himself, and if he does
not become utterly discouraged, he rouses himself to still
stronger effort and greater zeal. All this struggling is not
without its value and its use. It has its use, however, in
other ways than are commonly anticipated. It does the
very work that the law does—that is to say, it brings us
to the knowledge of our entire impotence; it leads us
to that despair of ourselves in which we become willing
to give to God the place that belongs to Him. This lesson
is entirely indispensable. "I can neither bestow this blessing on myself nor take it. It is God alone that must work
it in me."

The blessing of Pentecost is a supernatural gift, a wonderful act of God in the soul. The life of God in every
soul is just as truly a work of God as when that life was

first manifested in Jesus Christ. A Christian can do as little to bring the full life of the Spirit to fruition in his soul as the Virgin Mary did to conceive her supernatural child.[1] Like her, he can only receive it as the gift of God. The impartation of this heavenly blessing is as entirely an act of God as the resurrection of Christ from the dead was His divine work. As Christ Jesus had wholly and entirely to go down unto death, and lay aside utterly the life He had, in order to receive a new life from God, so must the believer abandon all power and hope of his own to receive this full blessing as a free gift of divine Omnipotence. This acknowledgment of our utter impotence, this descent into true self-despair, is indispensable if we would enjoy this supreme blessing.

V

I must have this blessing at any cost.

To get possession of the pearl of great price, the merchant man had to sell *all that he had*. The full blessing of Pentecost is to be obtained at no smaller price. He that would have it must sell all, must forsake all: sin to its smallest item, the love of the world in its most innocent forms, self-will in its simplest and most natural expressions, every faculty of our nature, every moment of our life, every pleasure that feeds our self-complacency, every exercise of our body, soul, and spirit—all must be surrendered to the power of the Spirit of God. In nothing can independent control or independent force have a place: everything—everything, I say—must be under the lead-

[1] Luke i. 38.

ing of the Spirit. One must indeed say: "Cost what it may, I am determined to have this blessing." Only the vessel that is utterly empty of everything can be filled and overflow with this living water.

We know that there is oftentimes a great gulf betwixt the will and the deed. Even when God has wrought the willing, the doing does not always come at once. But it will come wherever a man surrenders himself to the will which God has wrought, and openly expresses his consent in the presence of God. This, accordingly, is what must be done by the soul who intends to be sincerely ready to part with everything, even though he feels that he has no power to accomplish it. The selling price is not always paid at the moment; nevertheless, the purchaser may become the possessor as soon as the sale is concluded and security is given for the payment. O my brother, this very day speak the word: "Cost what it may, I will have this blessing." Jesus is surety that you will have power to abandon everything. Express your decision in the presence of God with confidence and perseverance. Repeat it before your own conscience and say: "I am a purchaser of the pearl of great price: I have offered everything to obtain the full blessing of Pentecost. I have said to God that I must, I will have it. By this decision I abide. I must, I will have it."

VI

In faith that God accepts my surrender and bestows this blessing upon me, I appropriate it for myself.

There is a great difference betwixt the appropriation

of a blessing by faith and the actual experience of it. It is because Christians do not understand this that they often become discouraged, when they do not at once experience the feeling and the enjoyment of what is promised them. Whenever in response to the offer of Christ you have said that you forsake all, and count it but loss for the full blessing of Pentecost, then from that moment you have to believe that He receives your offer and that He bestows upon you the fulness of the Spirit. Yet it may easily be that you cannot at that crisis trace any marked change in your experience. It is as if everything in you remained in its old condition. Now, however, is just the very time to persevere in faith. Learn by faith to be as sure as if you had seen it written in heaven that God has accepted your surrender of everything as a certain and completed transaction. In this faith look upon yourself as a man who is known to God as one that has sold everything to obtain this heavenly treasure. Believe that God has in heaven bestowed upon you the fulness of the Spirit. In this faith regard yourself as on the way to know the full blessing also in feeling and experience. Believe that God will order this blessing to break forth and be revealed in you. In this faith let your life be a life of joyful thanksgiving and expectation. God will not disappoint you.

VII

Now I count upon God and wait upon Him to reveal truly within me the blessing which He has bestowed upon me.

Faith must lead me to the actual inheritance of the pro-

c

mise, to the experience and enjoyment of it. Do not rest content with a belief that does not lead to experience. Rest in God by faith in the full assurance that He can make Himself known to you in a manner that is truly divine. At times the whole process may appear to you too great and too wonderful, and really impossible. Be not afraid. The more clearly you discern the amazing elements in the fact that you on your part have said to the Eternal Holy God that He on His part may have you to make you full of His Holy Spirit here on earth, the more shall you feel what a miracle of the grace of God it must be. There may be in you things you are not aware of, which hinder the breaking forth of the blessing. God is bent on putting them aside. Let them be consumed in the fire of strong burning desire. Let them be annihilated in the flame of God's countenance and His love. Let your expectation be fixed upon the Lord your God. He who in a frail woman revealed the divine life in the Infant Jesus, He that raised up the dead Jesus to the life of glory, He can—He will, indeed—just as miraculously bring this heavenly blessing to fruition in you, so that you may be filled with the Holy Spirit and that you may know, not by reasoning but by experience, that you have actually received the Holy Spirit.

Beloved brother, thou who readest all this, give answer, I entreat thee, to the summons I bring thee. God promises, God desires to make you full of the Holy Spirit. He would fain have your whole nature and life under the power of the Holy Spirit. He asks if you on your part are willing, if you really desire to have it. Pray let there be in your answer no uncertain sound, but let all that is within you cry out: "Yea, Lord, with all my heart." Let this promise of your God become the chief element in your life, the most precious, the chief, the only thing you seek. Do not be content to think and pray over it, but this very day enter into a transaction and a compact with God that will admit of no doubt concerning the choice you have made.

When once you have made this choice, cleave firmly to what is the chief element in it—namely, the faith that expects this blessing as a miracle of divine Omnipotence. The more earnestly you exercise that faith, the more will it teach you that your heart must be entirely emptied of verything and set free from every fetter, to be filled with the Spirit, to be occupied by the indwelling Christ. Contemplate yourself in faith as a man betwixt whom and God a firm compact has been made that you must receive the full blessing. You may take it for granted that it will surely come. Amen.

CHAPTER VII

HOW IT MAY BE KEPT

"But ye, praying in the Holy Spirit, keep yourselves in the love of God . . . Now unto Him who is able to guard you from stumbling, to the only God our Saviour, be glory for evermore. Amen."—Jude 21, 24.

CAN one who has the full blessing of Pentecost lose it again? Yes: undoubtedly. God does not bestow this boon with such constraint that a man retains it whether he will or not. No: this blessing also is intrusted to him as a talent which must be used; and only by use does it become secure and win success. Just as the Lord Jesus after He was baptized with the Holy Spirit had to be perfected by obedience and submission to the leading of the Spirit, so the Christian who has received the blessing of Pentecost has to see to it that he guards safely the deposit that has been intrusted to him.

When we inquire how we can keep it, Scripture points us to the fact that our keeping of it consists in our intrusting it to the Lord to be kept by Him. Paul places these two ideas alongside one another in his second letter to Timothy: "He is able to keep my deposit" (R.V. margin); "That good thing which was committed unto thee, guard through the Holy Spirit which dwelleth in us."[1] Jude also,

[1] Tim. i. 12, 14.

after saying, "Keep yourselves in the love of God," adds the doxology: "Unto Him that is able to keep us be glory."[1] The main secret of success in the preservation of the blessing is the exercise of a humble dependence on the Lord who keeps us and on the Spirit by whom we ourselves are kept in close fellowship with Him. It is with this blessing as with the manna that fell in the wilderness: it must be renewed from heaven every day. It is with the new heavenly life as with the life we live on earth: the fresh air that sustains it must be drawn in every moment from without and from above. Let us see how this ever-abiding, uninterrupted keeping takes place.

I

Jesus, who gave us the blessing, will keep it for us.

Jesus is the Keeper of Israel. This is His name and this is His work. God not only created the world but also keeps and upholds it. Jesus is not content with merely giving the blessing of Pentecost: He will also maintain it every moment. The Holy Spirit is not a power that in any sense is subordinate to us, that is intrusted to us, and that we must use; He is a power that is over and above us, that possesses and energises us, a power by which Jesus in heaven will carry forward His work from moment to moment. Our right place and our proper attitude must always be that of the deepest dependence, a sinking down in our own nothingness and impotence. Our chief concern is to let Jesus do His work within us.

So long as the soul does not discern this truth there will

[1] Jude 21, 24.

always be in it a certain dread of receiving the full blessing. Such a one will be inclined to say: "I shall not be able to continue in that holy life. I shall not be able to dwell always on such a lofty plane." But these thoughts only show what a feeble grasp such a one has of the great reality. When Jesus comes by the Spirit to dwell in my heart and to live in me, He will actually work out the maintenance of the blessing and regard my whole inner life as His special care. He who believes this truth sees that the life in the joy of the blessing of Pentecost, while it can never be relieved of the necessity of watchfulness, is a life that is freed from anxiety and ought to be characterized by continued gladness. The Lord has come into His holy temple. There He will abide and work out everything. He desires only this one thing—namely, that the soul shall know and honour Him as its faithful Shepherd, its Almighty Keeper. Jesus, who gives the blessing of Pentecost, will certainly keep it in us.

II

Jesus will keep the blessing, as He gave it, by faith.

The law that prevails at every stage in the progress of the kingdom of God is: "Be it unto you according to your faith." The faith that in the first reception of the Lord Jesus was as small as a grain of mustard-seed must, in the course of the Christian life, become always so enlarged that it shall see more and receive and enjoy more of the fulness that is in the Lord. Paul wrote to the Galatians: "I live, yet no longer I, but Christ liveth in me: and that life which I now live in the flesh I live in faith."[1] His faith

[1] Gal. ii. 20.

was as broad and boundless and unceasing as were the needs of his life and work. In everything and at all times, without ceasing, he trusted in Jesus to do all. His faith was as wide and abundant as the energy that flows from Jesus for the enrichment of His people is mighty and glorious. He had given up his whole life to Jesus: he himself lived no longer. By a continuous and unrestricted faith he gave to Jesus the liberty of energising his life without ceasing and without limitation.

The fulness of the Spirit is not a gift that is bestowed once for all as a part of the heavenly life. No: it is not so. It is rather a constantly flowing stream of the river of the water of life that issues from beneath the throne of God and of the Lamb. It is an uninterrupted communication of the life and the love of Jesus, the most personal and intimate association of the Lord with His own upon the earth. It is by the faith which discerns this truth, and assents to it, and cleaves to it with joy, that Jesus will certainly do His work of keeping.

III

Jesus keeps this blessing in fellowship with Himself.

The single aim of the blessing of Pentecost is to reveal Jesus as a Saviour, so that He may exhibit His power to redeem souls in us and by us here in the world. The Spirit did not come merely to occupy the place of Jesus, but only and wholly to unite the disciples with their Lord more closely, and deeply, and completely than when He was on earth. The power from on high did not come as a power which they were thenceforth to reckon as their own: the power was inseparably bound up with the Lord Jesus and the Holy Spirit. Every operation of the power was a direct working of God in them. The intercourse which the disciples had with Jesus on earth, the following of Him, the reception of His teaching, the doing of His will, the participation in His suffering—all this was to be still their experience, only in greater measure.

Not otherwise, accordingly, is it with us. The Spirit in us will always glorify Jesus, will always make it manifest that He alone is to be Lord, that all which is glorious comes only from Him. Close communion with God in the inner chamber, faithfulness in searching His Word and seeking to know His will in the Scriptures, sacrifice of time and business and intercourse with men, to bring us into touch with the Saviour—all this is indispensable for the keeping of the blessing. Jesus keeps us through our intercourse with Him, being occupied with Himself. He that loves His fellowship above everything shall have the experience of His keeping.

IV

Jesus keeps the blessing in the pathway of obedience.

When the Lord Jesus promised the Holy Spirit, He said three times over that the blessing was for the obedient. "If ye love Me, ye will keep My commandments : and I will pray the Father, and He shall give you another Comforter."[1] Peter speaks of "the Holy Spirit whom God hath given to them that obey Him."[2] Of our Lord Himself we read that "He became obedient unto death. Wherefore

---

[1] John xiv. 15, 16; cf. vv. 21, 23.   [2] Acts v. 32.

also God highly exalted Him." Obedience is what God cannot but demand. It is the only true relation and blessedness of the creature. It is obedience that attains what was lost by the Fall. It is the power of obedience Jesus came to restore. It is His own life. Apart from obedience the blessing of Pentecost can neither come nor abide.

There are two kinds of obedience. There is one that is very defective, like that of the disciples previously to Pentecost. They desired from the heart to do what the Lord said, but they had not the power. Yet the Lord accounted their desire and purpose as obedience. On the other hand, there is a more abundant life, which comes with the fulness of the Spirit, where new power is given for full obedience. The characteristic of the full blessing of Pentecost, and the way to keep it, is a surrender to obedience in the minutest details. To listen to the voice of Jesus Himself, to the voice of the Spirit, to the voice of Conscience, this is the way in which Jesus leads us. The method of making the life of Pentecost within us sure and strong is to know Jesus and to love Him, and receive Him in that aspect which made Him well-pleasing to the Father—namely, as the Obedient One. The whole Jesus becomes the life of the soul.

It is the exercise of this obedience that gives to the soul a wonderful firmness and confidence and power to trust God and to expect all from Him. A strong will is necessary for a strong faith, and it is in obedience that the will is strengthened to trust God to the uttermost. This is the only way in which the Lord can lead us to ever richer blessing.

V

Jesus keeps the blessing in fellowship with His people.

At the outset of His seeking for the full blessing a Christian thinks for the most part only of himself. Even after he receives the blessing as a new experience, he is still rather disposed to see merely how he can keep it safely for himself. But very speedily the Spirit will teach him that a member of the body cannot enjoy the flow of healthful life in a state of separation from others. He begins to understand that "there is one body and one Spirit." The unity of the body must be realized to enjoy the fulness of the Spirit.

This principle teaches us some very important lessons about the condition on which the blessing received can be maintained. All that you have belongs to others, and must be employed for their service. All that they have belongs to you, and is in turn indispensable for you. The Spirit of the body of the Lord can work effectively only when the members of it work in unison. You should confess to others what the Lord has done for you, ask their intercession, seek their fellowship, and help them with what the Lord has given you. You should lay to heart the unhappy condition of the enfeebled Christian Church in our days, yet not in the spirit of judgment or bitterness, but rather in the spirit of humility and prayer, of gentleness and willingness to serve. Jesus will teach you what is meant by the saying that "love is the greatest";[1] and by the very intensity of your surrender to the welfare of His Church He will both keep and increase the blessing in you.

[1] 1 Cor. xiii. 13.

VI

Jesus keeps the blessing in the service of His kingdom.

We have said more than once that the Spirit came as the power for work. The very name of Jesus Christ involves entire consecration to God's work, utter devotion to the rescue of souls. It was for this end alone that He lived: it is only for this cause that He lives in heaven. How can anyone ever dream of having the Spirit of Christ otherwise than as a Spirit which aims at the work of God and the salvation of souls? It is an impossibility. Hence from the outset we must keep these two aspects of the Spirit's operation closely knit together. What the Spirit works in us is for the sake of what He works by us. Our seeking for the blessing will miscarry, our initial possession of the blessing will be lost, if we do not as the dominant feature of our life present ourselves to be used by the Spirit in the doing of His work.

The blessing of Pentecost does not always come with equal power and not always at once. God often gives preparatory experiences and awakenings that must lead to the full blessing. Every attempt to keep such gracious gifts for ourselves will entail loss. He that does not follow his own inclination, either in being silent or in speaking, but presents himself to the Lord and waits upon Him with an undivided spirit, will experience that work, so far from exhausting or weakening, is the sure way to keep the treasure.

VII

One thought more. *It is as the indwelling Lord that Jesus keeps the blessing of Pentecost in us.*

Whenever mention is made of Jesus as our Keeper, it is oftentimes difficult to believe that we who are upon the earth can really know ourselves to be always, without interruption, in His hands and under His power. How much clearer and more glorious does the truth become when the Spirit discovers to us that Christ is in us; and that, not only as a tenant in a house, or water in a glass, in such a fashion that they continue quite distinct, but rather as the soul is in the body animating and moving every part of it, and never to be separated from each other except by a violent death. Yes : it is thus that Christ dwells in us, penetrating our whole nature with His nature. The Holy Spirit came for the purpose of making Him thus deeply present within us. As the sun is high in the firmament above me, and yet by his heat penetrates my bones and marrow and quickens my whole life, so the Lord Jesus, who is exalted high in heaven, penetrates my whole nature by His Spirit in such a way, that all my willing, and thinking, and feeling are animated by Him. Once this fact is fully grasped, we no longer think of an external keeping through a person outside of us in heaven, but rather become convinced that our whole individual life is itself quickened and possessed by One who, not in a human but in a divine, all-penetrating manner, occupies and fills the heart. Then we see how natural, how certain, how blessed it is that the indwelling Jesus keeps the blessing and always maintains the fulness of the Spirit.

Brethren, is there anyone amongst you who is longing for this life in the fulness of blessing, and yet is afraid to enter upon it, because he knows not how he is to persevere? Pray listen to what I say: Jesus will make this blessing continuous and sure. Is there any one of you who longs for it and yet cannot understand wherein the secret of it lies? Again listen to me: the blessing is this—that as Jesus Christ was daily with His disciples in bodily fashion, so He will by His Spirit every day and always be your life; yea, live His life in you. No one can fully understand how things look on the top of a mountain until he himself has been there. Although you do not understand everything, yet believe that the Lord Jesus has sent His Spirit with no other object in view than just to receive and keep you in His divine power. Trust Him for this. Let all burdens be laid aside, and give yourself up to receive from Him this full blessing of Pentecost as a fountain which He Himself will cause to spring up in you unto everlasting life.

CHAPTER VIII

HOW IT MAY BE INCREASED

"He that believeth on Me shall never thirst."—
John vi. 35.

*"He that believeth on Me, out of him shall flow rivers of
living water."*—John vii. 38.

CAN the full blessing of Pentecost be still further
increased? Can anything that is full become still fuller?
Yes: undoubtedly. It can become so full that it always
overflows. This is especially the characteristic and law of
the blessing of Pentecost.

The words of our blessed Lord Jesus which have been
quoted, point us to a double blessing. First, Jesus says that
he who believes in Him shall never thirst: he shall always
have life in himself—that is to say, the satisfaction of all
his needs. Then He speaks of something that is grander
and more glorious: he that believeth in Him, out of his
heart shall flow rivers of living water to quench the thirst
of others. It is the distinction betwixt full and overflowing.
A vessel may be full and yet have nothing over for others.
When it continues full, and yet has something over for
others, there must be in it an over-brimming, ever-flowing
supply. This is what our Lord promises to His believing
disciples. At the outset, faith in Him gives them the blessing that they shall never thirst. But as they advance and

become stronger in faith, it makes them a fountain of water out of which streams flow to others. The Spirit who at first only fills us will overflow out of us to souls around us.

It is with the rivers of living water as with many a fountain on earth. When we begin to open them, the stream is weak. The more the water is used, and the more deeply the source is opened up, the more strongly does the water flow. I should like to inquire how far this principle holds good in the realm of the spiritual life and to discover what is necessary to secure that the fulness of the Spirit may constantly flow more abundantly from us. There are several simple directions which may help us in reaching this knowledge.

I

Hold fast that which you have.

See to it that you do not misunderstand the blessing which God has given you. Be sure that you do not form any wrong conceptions of what the full blessing is. Do not imagine that the animation, and joy, and power of Pentecost must be felt and seen immediately. No: the Church at present is in a dead-and-alive condition, and the restoration often comes slowly. At first, indeed, one receives the full blessing only as a seed: the full life is wrapt up in a little invisible capsule. The quickened soul has longed for it; he has surrendered himself unreservedly for it; he has believed in silence that God has accepted his consecration and fulfilled His promise. In that faith he goes on his way, silent and happy, saying to himself: "The blessing of the fulness of the Spirit is for me." But the actual experiences of the blessing did not come as he had anticipated; or they did come, but lasted only for a short time. The result was that he began to fear that his surrender was not a reality; that he had been rejoicing in what was only a transient emotion; and that the real blessing was something greater and more powerful than he had yet received. The result is that very speedily the blessing becomes less instead of larger, and he moves farther back rather than forward through discouragement on account of his disappointment.

The cause of this condition is simply lack of faith. We are bent on judging God and His work in us by sight and feeling. We forget that the whole process is the work of faith. Even in its highest revelations in Christians that have made the greatest progress, faith rests not on what is to be seen of the work of God or on the experiences of it, but on the work of God as spiritual, invisible, deeply hidden, and inconceivable. To you, therefore, my brother, who desirest in this time of discouragement to return to the true life according to the promise, my counsel is not to be greatly surprised if it comes to you slowly or if it appears to be involved in darkness. If you know that you have given yourself to God with a perfect heart, and if you know that God, really and with His whole heart, waits to fulfil His promise in you with divine power, then rest in silence before His face and hold fast your integrity. Although the cold of winter appears to bury everything in death, say with the prophet Habakkuk: "Though the fig-tree shall not blossom, neither shall fruit be in the vines, yet I will rejoice in the Lord, I will joy in the God of my salvation."[1]

[1] Hab. iii. 17.

Do this, and you shall know God, and God will know you. If you are sure that you have set yourself before God as an empty, separated, purified vessel, to become full of His Spirit, then continue still to regard yourself so and keep silence before Him. If you have believed that God has received you to fill you as a purified vessel—purified through Jesus Christ and by your entire surrender to Him —then abide in this attitude day by day, and you may reckon upon it that the blessing will grow and begin to flow. "He that believeth shall not be ashamed."[1]

II

Persevere in the entire denial of yourself and the sacrifice of everything.

If I wish to have a reservoir of water, the greater the excavation I make for it, the wider the space I occupy with it, the greater is the quantity of water I can collect, and the stronger is the stream that flows from it when the sluices are opened. In your surrender for sanctification, or for the full blessing of the Spirit, you have said in truth and uprightness that you are prepared to sacrifice and forsake all in order to win this pearl of the kingdom of heaven; and this consecration was acceptable to God. But you have not yet fully understood the full import of the words you have used. The Lord has still much to teach you concerning what the individual self is, how deeply rooted in your nature, how utterly corrupt as well as deeply hidden it is, as the secret source of many things you both say and do. Be willing to make room for the Spirit by a constant, daily,

[1] Isa. xxviii. 16; 1 Pet. ii. 6.

and entire denial of the self-life, and you may be sure that He will always be willing to come and fill the empty place. You have forsaken and sacrificed everything so far as you know; but keep your mind open to the teaching of the Spirit, and He will lead you farther on, and let you see that only when the entire sacrifice of everything after the example of Christ comes to be the rule in His Church, shall the blessing again break forth like an overflowing stream.

It is surprising how sometimes a very little thing may hinder the continuance in the increase of the blessing. It may, for example, be a little variance betwixt friends, in which they show that they are not willing to forgive and forbear at once according to the law of Christ. Or it may be some unobserved yielding to undue sensitiveness or to the ambition which is not prepared to take the lowest place. Or it may be the possession or use of earthly property as if it were our own. Or it may be some providing for the flesh in the enjoyment of eating and drinking without the self-denial which Christ always expects at our hands every day. Or it may be in connection with things that are lawful and in themselves innocent, which however, do not befit us in our profession of being led by the Spirit of God. For here, like the Lord Jesus in His poverty, we are bound to show that the heavenly portion we possess is itself sufficient to satisfy all our desires. Or it may be in connection with doubtful things, in which we give way too easily to the lust of the flesh.

Christian brother, do you really desire to enjoy the full measure of the blessing of the Spirit? Then, before temptation comes, train yourself to understand the fundamental law of the imitation of Jesus and of full discipleship—

namely, *Forsake all*. Suffer yourself also to be strengthened and drawn into the observance of it by the sure promise of the "hundredfold in this life." A full blessing will be given you, a measure shaken together and running over.

III

Regard yourself as living only to make others happy.

God is Love. His whole being is nothing but a surrender of Himself in love to be the life of the creature, to make the creature participate in His holiness and blessedness. He blesses and serves all that lives. His glory as God is that He puts all that He has at the disposal of His creatures.

Jesus Christ is the Son of God's love, the Bearer, the Bringer, the Dispenser of the love. What God is as invisible in heaven, He was as visible on earth. He came, He lived, He suffered and died only to glorify the Father— that is, to let it be seen how glorious the Father in His love is, and to show that in the Godhead there is no other pur- pose than to bless men and make them happy; to make it manifest that the highest honour and blessedness of any being is to give and to sacrifice.

The Holy Spirit came as the Spirit of the Father and the Son to make us partakers of this divine nature, to shed abroad the love of God in our hearts, to secure the indwell- ing of the Son and His love in our hearts to such an extent that Christ may verily be formed within us, and that our whole "inner man" shall bear the impress of His disposition and His likeness.

Hence, when any soul seeks and receives the fulness of the Spirit, and desires to have it increased, is it not perfectly evident that he can enjoy this blessing only according as he is prepared to give himself to a life in the service of love? The Spirit comes to expel the life of self and self-seeking. The fulness of the Spirit presupposes a willingness to consecrate ourselves to the blessing of others and as the servants of all, and that in a constantly increasing and unreserved measure. The Spirit is the outflowing of the life of God. If we will but yield ourselves to Him, He will become rivers of living water, flowing from the depths of our heart.

Christian brother, if you will have the blessing increased, begin to live as a man who is left here on earth only in order that the love of God may work by you. Love all around you with the love of God which is in you through the Spirit. Love the children of God cordially, even the weakest and most perverse. Exercise and exihibit your love in every possible way. Love the unsaved. Present yourself to the Spirit to love Him. Then will love constrain you to speak, to work, to give, and to pray. If there is no open door for working, or if you have not the strength for it, the door of prayer is always open, and power can be obtained at the mercy-seat. Embrace the whole world in your love; for Christ, who is in your heart, belongs also to the heathen. The Spirit is the power of Christ for redeeming them. Like God and Jesus and the Spirit, live wholly to bless others. Then the blessing shall stream forth and become overflowing.

IV

Let Jesus Christ for your faith be everything.

You know what the Scripture says: "It was the good

pleasure of the Father than IN HIM should all the fulness dwell, that in all things HE might have the preeminence";[1] and again : "All the promises of God are IN HIM Yea, and IN HIM Amen, to the glory of God by us."[2] When the Lord spoke of "rivers of living water," He connected the promise with faith in Himself : "He that believeth in ME, out of his heart shall flow rivers." If we only understood that word "believeth" rightly, we should require no other answer than this to the question as to how the blessing may be increased.

Faith is primarily a seeing by the Spirit that Jesus is nothing but a flowing fountain of the divine love, and that the Spirit Himself always flows from Him as the Bearer of the life that this love brings and that always streams forth in love. Then it is an embracing of the promise, an appropriation of the blessing as it is provided in Christ, a resting in the certainty of it, and a thanking of God for what He is yet to do. Thereafter, faith is a keeping open of the soul, so that Christ can come in with the blessing and take possession and fill all. Faith becomes the most fervent and unbroken communion betwixt the soul in which Christ obtains His place and Christ Himself, who by the silent, effectual blessing of the Spirit is enthroned in the heart.

Christian brother, pray, learn the lesson that, if you believe, you shall see the glory of God. Let every doubt, every weakness, every temptation find you trusting, rejoicing in Jesus, and reckoning upon Him always to work all in you. You know that there are two ways in which a believer can encounter and strive against sin. One is to endeavour to ward it off with all his might, seeking his

[1] Cor. i. 19.   [2] 2 Cor. i. 20.

strength in the Word and in prayer. In this form of the conflict we use the power of the will. The other is to turn at the very moment of the temptation to the Lord Jesus in the silent exercise of faith and say to Him: "Lord, I have no strength. THOU art my Keeper."[1] This is the method of faith. "This is the victory that overcometh the world, even your faith."[2] Yes: this is indeed "the one thing needful," because it is the only way in which Jesus, who is in Himself "The One Thing Needful," can maintain the work of His Spirit in us. It is by the exercise of faith without ceasing that the blessing will flow without ceasing.

Christ must be all to us every moment. It is of no avail to me that I have life on earth unless that life is renewed every moment by my inbreathing of fresh air. Even so must God actually renew, and uphold, and strengthen the divine life in me every moment. He does this for me in my union with Christ. Christ is simply the fulness of God, the life of God, the love of God prepared for us and communicating itself to us. The Spirit is simply the fulness of Christ, the life of Christ, the self-communicating love of Christ, surrounding us as the air surrounds the body.

O let us believe that we are in Christ, who surrounds us in His heavenly power, longing to make the rivers of His Spirit flow forth by us! Let us endeavour to obtain a heart filled with the joyful assurance that the Almighty Lord will fulfil His word with power, and that our only choice is to see Him, to rejoice in Him, and sacrifice all for Him. Then shall His word become true: "He that believeth in Me, out of his heart shall flow rivers of living water." Amen.

[1] Ps. cxxi. 5.   [2] 1 John v. 4.

CHAPTER IX

HOW IT COMES TO ITS FULL MANIFESTATION

"I bow my knees unto the Father"—

1. *That He would grant you that ye may be strengthened with power through His Spirit in the inward man;*
2. *That Christ may dwell in your hearts through faith;*
3. *That ye, being rooted and grounded in love, may be strong to know the love of Christ which passeth knowledge;*
4. *That ye may be filled unto all the fulness of God.*
   —Eph. iii. 14-19.

WE have remarked several times that every blessing which God gives is like a seed with the power of an indissoluble life hidden in it. Let no one therefore imagine that to be filled with the Spirit is a condition of perfectness which leaves nothing more to be desired. In no sense can this be true. It was after the Lord Jesus was filled with the Spirit at His baptism He had to go forth to be still further perfected by temptations and the learning of obedience. When the disciples were filled with the Spirit on the day of Pentecost, this equipment with power from on high was given to them that they might carry out the victory over sin in their own lives and all around them. The Spirit is the

Spirit of truth, and He must guide us into it. It will only be by slow degrees that He will lead us into the eternal purpose of God, into the knowledge of Christ, into true holiness, into full fellowship with God. The fulness of the Spirit is simply the full preparation for living and working as a child of God.

When we consider the matter from this point of view, we see at a glance how entirely indispensable it is for every child of God to aim at obtaining this blessing. Then we begin to feel that this is the very blessing that is to be pressed on the acceptance of the weak and timid. We also understand why it is that Paul offers this prayer on which we are now to meditate, in behalf of all believers without distinction. He did not regard it as a spiritual distinction or special luxury which was intended only for those who were prominent or favoured amongst the children of God. No: it was for all without distinction, for all who at their conversion had by faith received the Holy Spirit, that he prayed. And his request was that by the special, powerful, and ever-deepening work of the Spirit, God would bring them to what was their true destiny—namely, to be filled unto all the fulness of God. This prayer of Paul is everywhere regarded as one of the most glorious representations that the Word of God gives of what the life of a Christian ought to be. Let us then endeavour to learn what the full revelation and manifestation of this blessing of the Spirit may become.

I

That the Father would grant you that ye may be strengthened with power through the Spirit.

That these Christians had received the Spirit when they believed in Christ is clear from a previous statement of the Epistle.[1] But he sees that they do not yet know or have all that the Spirit can do for them, and that there is a danger that, by their ignorance, they may make no further progress. Hence he bows his knees and prays without ceasing in their behalf that the Father would strengthen them with might by His Spirit in the inner man. This powerful strengthening with the Spirit, is equivalent to being filled with the Spirit, is indeed this same blessing under another aspect. It is the indispensable condition of a healthful, growing, and fruitful life.

Paul prays that the Father would grant this boon. He asks for a new, definite operation of God. He entreats that God would do this *according to the riches of His glory.* It is surely not any trifling thing, anything very common, that he thus craves. He desires that God would remember and bring into play all the riches of His grace and, in a fashion commensurate with the divine glory of His power, do a heavenly wonder and as the living God strengthen these believers with might by His Spirit in the inner man.

O Christian, learn at this point that your life every day depends on God's will, on God's grace, on God's omnipotence. Yes: every moment God must work in your inner life and strengthen you by His Spirit, otherwise you cannot live as He would have you live. Just as no creature in the natural world can exist for a moment if God does not work in it to sustain its life, so the gift of the Holy Spirit is the pledge that God Himself is to work everything in us from

---

[1] Cf. chap. 1. ver. 14.

moment to moment. Learn to know your entire, your blessed dependence on God, and the claim which you have on Him as your Heavenly Father to begin in you a life in the mighty strengthening of the Spirit and to maintain it without the interruption of a single moment.

Paul tells these believers what he prays for in their behalf, in order that they may know what they have need of and ask it for themselves. Do you also learn to offer up this petition. Expect everything from God alone. Bow your knees, and ask and expect from the Father that He would manifest to you—yes, in you—the riches of His glory. Ask and expect that He would strengthen you with might by His Spirit, that Spirit who in fact is already in you, but only as an unknown, hidden, and slumbering seed. Let this become the one desire, the strong confidence of your soul: "God will fill me with the Spirit: God will strengthen me through the Spirit with His Almighty energy." Let your whole life every day be permeated by this prayer and this expectation.

II

That Christ may dwell in your hearts by faith.

This is the glorious fruit of the divine strengthening with might in the inner man by the Spirit. The great work of the Father in eternity is to bring forth the Son.

In Him alone is the good pleasure of God realized. The Father can have no fellowship with the creature except through the Son. He can have no joy in it except in so far as He beholds His Son in it. Hence it is His great work in redemption to reveal His Son in us, and so to obtain an abode for Him in us, that our life shall be a visible expression of the life of Jesus.

That is the aim He has in view in strengthening us with might by the Spirit in the inner man. It is that Christ may dwell in our hearts by faith.

This indwelling of Christ in us is not like that of a man who abides in a house, but is nevertheless in no sense identified with it. No: His indwelling is a possession of our hearts that is truly divine, quickening and penetrating their inmost being with His life. The Father strengthens us inwardly with might by His Spirit, so that the Spirit animates our will and brings it, like the will of Jesus, into entire sympathy with His own. The result is that our heart then, like the heart of Jesus, bows before Him in humility and surrender; our life seeks only His honour; and our whole soul thrills with desire and love for Jesus. This inward renewal makes the heart fit to be a dwelling place of the Lord. By the Spirit He is revealed within us and we come to know that He is actually in us as our life, in a deep, divine unity, One with us.

Brother, God longs to see Jesus in you. He is prepared to work mightily in you that Christ may dwell in you. The Spirit has come, and the Father is willing to work mightily by Him, that the living presence of His Son may always abide in you. Jesus loves you so dearly and longs so intensely for you that He cannot rest until He makes His abode in your heart. This is the supreme blessing that the fulness of the Spirit brings you.

That Christ may dwell in your heart by faith. It is by faith that you receive and know the indwelling of the Spirit and the operation of the Father by Him. By faith,

which discerns things invisible as clearly as the sun, you
receive and know the living Jesus in your heart. As constantly as He was with His disciples on earth—yea, more
constantly than with them, because more inwardly and
more really—He will be in you and will grant you to
enjoy His presence and His love. O soul, pray that the
Father would strengthen you with might by the Spirit,
would open your heart for the fulness of the Spirit, and
enable you trustfully to appropriate it. Then at last shall
you know what it means to have Christ dwelling in your
heart by faith.

III

*That ye, being rooted and grounded in love, may be
strong to know the love of Christ which passeth knowledge.*

Here is the glorious fruit of the indwelling of Christ
in the heart. By the Spirit the love of God is shed abroad
in the heart. By Christ who dwells in the heart the love
wherewith God loved Him comes into us; and we learn
that just as life in God, between Father, Son, and Spirit,
is only infinite love, so the life of Christ in us is nothing
but love. Thus we become rooted and grounded in love.
We are implanted in the soil of love: we strike our roots
into heavenly love; henceforth we have our being in it
and draw our strength from it. Love is the supreme
element in our spiritual life. The Spirit in us and the Son
in us bring us nothing but the love of God. Love is the
first and the chief among the streams of living water that
are to flow from us.

It is thus that we come to discover the truths that love is the fulfilling of the law; that love doeth no ill to one's neighbour;[1] that love seeketh not its own;[2] that love lays down its life for the brethren.[3] Our heart becomes ever larger and larger; our friends, our enemies, the children of God and the children of the world, those that are worthy to be loved and those that are hateful, the ransomed and the lost, the world as a whole and every individual creature in particular—are all embraced in the love of God. We find, then, our happiness lies in the sacrifice of our own honour, our own advantage and comfort, in favour of others. Love takes no account of sacrifice: it is its blessedness to love: it cannot do otherwise; actual loving is its nature and its life. We are able so to love, because the Father with His Spirit works mightily within us; because the Son, "who loved me and gave Himself for me," dwells in us, and He, who is crucified Love, has filled the heart completely with Himself. We are rooted in love, and in accordance with the nature of the root in God is the fruit from God—love.

That ye may be strong to know the love which passeth knowledge: that is, to know love not with the knowledge of the understanding and its thoughts alone, but in the conscious blessedness of a heart in which Jesus dwells; to know love as something that cannot be known or conceived by the heart of itself; to be strong to know it fully, so far as this is possible before God, in order that He may fill you, an earthen vessel, with His own love to overflowing.

O souls, pray, listen to the word: "God is Love"; and

[1] Rom. xiii. 1o.   [2] 1 Cor. xiii. 5.   [3] 1 John iii. 16.

He has provided everything to the end that you may know love fully. It is for this object that the Spirit is in you, and that the Father will work mightily in you: it is with this aim that Christ desires to have your whole heart. O let us begin to pray, as never before, that the Father would strengthen us with might by the Spirit; that the Father would grant unto us to be filled with the Spirit; that ye may be strong to know the love of Christ.

IV

That ye may be filled unto all the fulness of God.

What an expression! what an impenetrable mystery! what a divine blessedness! *Filled* unto all the fulness of God: this is the experience to which the fulness of the Spirit is intended to bring us, and will bring us.

Filled unto all the *fulness* of God: who shall ever unfold the meaning of this expression to us? How shall we ever reach any definite idea of what it signifies? God has made provision for our enlightenment. In Christ Jesus we see a man full of God, a man who was perfected by suffering and obedience, filled unto all the fulness of God: yea, a man who in the solitariness and poverty of an ordinary human life, with all its needs and infirmities, has nevertheless let us see on earth the life enjoyed by the inhabitants of heaven, as they are there filled unto all the fulness of God. The will and the honour, the love and the service of God were always visible in Him. God was all to Him.

When God called the world into existence it was in

order that it might reveal Him. In it His wisdom and might and goodness were to dwell and be visibly manifested. We say continually that nature is full of God. God can be seen in everything by the believing eye. The Seraphim sing: the whole earth is full of His glory. When God created man after His image, it was in order that He Himself might be seen in man, that man should simply serve as a reflection of His likeness. The image of a man never serves any other purpose than to represent the man. As the image of God man was destined simply to receive the glory of God in his own life, to bear it and make it visible. God was to be all to him; to be all in him: he was to be full of God.

By sin this divine purpose has been frustrated. Instead of being full of God, man became full of himself and the world; and to such an extent has sin blinded us that it appears an impossibility ever to become full of God again. Alas! even many Christians see nothing desirable in this fulness. Yet it is back to this blessing that Jesus came to redeem and bring us; and this is the end for which God is prepared to work mightily within us by His Spirit. This is no less the result for which the Son of God desires to dwell in our heart, and which He will bring to accomplishment: it is all that we may be filled unto the fulness of God.

Yes; this is the highest aim of the Pentecostal blessing. To attain this, we can count upon the Spirit to make sure of our reaching it. He will open the way for us and guide us in it. He will work in us the deep humility of Jesus, who always said: "I can of Myself do *nothing*"; "I do *not* My own will"; "The words I speak, I speak *not* of

Myself."[1] Amidst this self-emptying and sense of dependence He will work in us the assurance and the experience that for the soul which is nothing, God is surely ALL. By our faith He will reveal to us Jesus, who was full of God, as our life. He will cause us to be rooted in the love in which God gives all, and we shall take God as all. Thus it will be with us as with Jesus: man nothing, and God's honour, God's will, God's love, God's power, everything. Yes; the issue will be that we shall be "filled unto all the fulness of God."

Christian, I beg of you by the love of God not to say that this is too high an experience for you, or that it is not for you. No; it is in truth the will of God concerning you: the will alike of His commandment and of His promise. He is bent on fulfilling His promise: He Himself will work it out. To-day, then, in humility and faith take this word, "FILLED UNTO ALL THE FULNESS OF GOD," as the purpose and the watchword of your life, and see what it will do for you. It will become to you a mighty lever to raise you out of the self-seeking which is quite content with only being prepared for blessing. It will urge you to enter into and become firmly rooted in the love of God which gives everything to you, and thereby in the love which gives everything back to Him. It will convince you, that nothing less than Christ Himself dwelling in your heart can keep such a love abiding in you, or actually make the fulness of God a reality within you. It will train you to fix your only hope of all this blessing on the mighty operation of God Himself by the Spirit. It will also move you to go down upon your knees and

[1] John v. 30, vi. 38, xii. 49, xiv. 10.

summon to your aid the wealth of God's glory, that it may itself prepare you for this great wonder. This it will continue to do until your heart is enabled to utter the response: "Yes: FILLED UNTO ALL THE FULNESS OF GOD is what my God has prepared for me."

With this glorious prospect before us, come and let us join with the apostle in the doxology: "Unto Him that is able to do exceeding abundantly above all that we ask or think, according to the power that worketh in us (the power of His might), unto Him be the glory for ever and ever."[1] Let us desire nothing less than these riches of the glory of God. To-day, if we have never done it before, let us make a beginning and appropriate to ourselves the full blessing of the Spirit as the power which is sure to lead us to be "filled unto all the fulness of God."

When God said to Abraham, "I am God Almighty," He invited him to trust His omnipotence to fulfil His promise. When Jesus went down into the grave and its impotence, it was in the faith that God's omnipotence could lift Him to the throne of His glory. It is that same Omnipotence that waits to work out God's purpose in them that believe in Him to do so. Let our hearts say, "Unto Him THAT IS ABLE to do exceeding abundantly above all that we ask or think, unto Him be the glory." Amen.

[1] Eph. iii. 20, 21.

D

CHAPTER X

HOW FULLY IT IS ASSURED TO US BY GOD

"If ye then, being evil, know how to give good gifts to your children, how much more shall your Heavenly Father give the Holy Spirit to them that ask Him?"—Luke xi. 13.

WHEN Jairus came to the Lord Jesus to entreat His help for his dying daughter, and he learned by the way the sorrowful tidings that she had already died, Jesus said: "Be not afraid: only believe."[1] Face to face with a trial in which man was utterly helpless, the Lord called upon him to put his trust in Himself. There was but one thing that suited his case or could help him: "only believe." Many a thousand times has that word been the strength of God's children, where so far as man was concerned all hope was lost and success appeared to be impossible. So here also, whilst we are on our way to search for and know the full Pentecostal blessing, we have need of this word. In view of the inconceivable preciousness of the blessing, and of the divine element in it, it will indeed be only the wonder-working power of God that can make this exceeding grace a reality within us. Let us only be silent before God; here also we shall hear the voice of Jesus saying to us: "Be not afraid, only believe: God will do it for you."

[1] Luke viii. 50.

It is nothing less than this that is the aim of this word of our Lord concerning the divine assurance that, much more readily than an earthly father will give his children bread, will God give the Holy Spirit to them that ask Him. We should regard it as quite unnatural on the part of a father if he did not give his child bread; how much more, then, shall not God give the Holy Spirit, yea, all the promised fulness of the Spirit, to those that ask Him. In the midst of all our thinking and speaking, all our praying and hoping, the fundamental element in our spiritual life must be the firm confidence that the Father will give His child His full heritage. God is spirit: He desires in His eternal love to obtain full possession of us; but He can do this in no other manner than by giving us His Spirit. As surely as He is God, will He, O child of God, fill thee with His Holy Spirit. Without that faith you will never succeed in your quest of this blessing. That faith will give you the victory over every difficulty. Therefore, "be not afraid: only believe." Hear the voice of Jesus: "Said I not unto thee that if thou believest thou shalt see the glory of God?"

Let us listen to these three great lessons.

I

Although you cannot comprehend or explain everything by the mere power of your understanding, still: "only believe."

There are many preliminary questions which arise at once in connection with this subject, and which tempt us to resolve that we shall first take in and understand everything about it before we expect the blessing. Two of these questions I shall venture to mention now.

The first is: whence must this blessing come, from WITHIN or from ABOVE? Some earnest Christians will say at once that "it must come from WITHIN." The Holy Spirit descended upon the earth on the day of Pentecost and was given to the Christian community. At the moment of conversion He comes into our heart. We have therefore no longer to pray that He may be given to us: we have simply to recognize and use what we already have. It is not as if we had to seek to have more of the Spirit: we have Him in the fulness of the gift as it is. It is rather the Holy Spirit who must have more of us. As we yield ourselves entirely to Him He will entirely fill us. It is from WITHIN that the blessing must come: the fountain of living water is already there; the fountain has only to be open and every obstruction cleared and the water shall stream forth.   It must spring from WITHIN.

On the other hand, there are not a few that say, "No; it must come from ABOVE." When, on the arrival of the day of Pentecost, the Father bestowed the Spirit, He did not give Him away beyond His own control. The fulness of the Spirit still remains in God. God bestows nothing apart from Himself, to work without or independently of His will. He Himself works only through the Spirit and every new and greater manifestation of the Spirit's power comes directly from ABOVE. Long after the day of Pentecost the Spirit came down again from heaven at Samaria and Cæsarea. In His fulness He is in heaven still; and it is from God in heaven that the fulness of the Spirit is to be ever waited for.

Brother Christian, pray, do not linger till by reasonings of your own you have decided which of these representations is the right one. God can bless men in both ways When the flood came all the fountains of the abyss were broken up and the sluices of heaven were opened. It came simultaneously from beneath and from above. God is prepared to bless men in both of these methods. He desires to teach us to know and honour the Spirit who is already within us. He would fain also bring us to wait upon Himself in a spirit of utter dependence, and to beseech Him that He as our Father would give us our daily bread, the new, the fuller influx of His Spirit. I entreat you not to suffer yourself to be held back by such a question as this. God understands your petition. He knows what you would have. Believe that God is prepared to fill you with His Spirit; let that faith look up to Him with unceasing prayer and confidence. He will give the blessing.

The other question is: Does this blessing come gradually or at once? Will it manifest itself in the shape of a silent, unobserved increase of the grace of the Spirit or as a momentary, immediate outpouring of His power? It must suffice for me to say here again that God has already sent this blessing in both modes, and will continue to do so still. What must take place at once is this: there must be a definite desolve to place the whole life unreservedly under the control of the Spirit, and a conviction of faith that God has accepted this surrender. In the majority of cases this is done at once. It must at last come to this, perhaps after a long course of seeking and praying that the soul shall present itself to God for this blessing in one definite, irrevocable act, and shall believe that the offering is then sanctified and accepted upon the altar. Thenceforth, whether the experience of the blessing comes at once and with power, or comes quietly and gradually, the soul must maintain its act of self-dedication and simply look to God to do His own work.

Thus in dealing with all such questions the chief concern is this: "only believe" and rest in the FAITHFULNESS OF GOD. Hold fast this one principle: God has given us a promise that He will fill us with His Spirit. It is His work to make His promise an accomplished fact. Thank God for the promise even as you would thank Him for the fulfilment of it. In the promise God has already pledged Himself to you. Rejoice in Him and in His faithfulness. Be not held back by any questions whatever. Set your heart on what God will do, on Himself from whom the blessing must come. The result will be certain and glorious.

II

Although you receive but little help from others, or even encounter opposition, still: "only believe."

It is one of the saddest tokens of the unspiritual condition of the Church that so many are content with things just as they are, and have no desire to know more of this seeking for the reality of the Spirit's power. They point to the present purity of doctrine, to the prevailing earnestness of preaching, to the generous gifts which are made for the maintenance of religious works and the enterprises of philanthropy, to the interest which is manifested in the cause of education and of missions, and they say that we ought rather to give God thanks for the good we see around us. Such people would condemn the language of Laodicea, and would refuse to say that they were rich and increased in goods and had need of nothing,[1] and yet there are some traces of this spirit in what they say. They do not consider the injunction to be "filled with the Spirit." They have forgotten the command to prophesy to the Spirit and say: "Come from the four winds, O Breath, and breathe upon the slain, that they may live."[2] When you speak of these things you will receive little encouragement from them. They do not understand what you mean. They believe indeed in the Holy Spirit, but their eyes have not been opened to the fact that more of the Spirit, the fulness of the Spirit, is the one thing needful for the Church.

There are others who will agree with you when you speak of this need, and yet will really give you even less encouragement. They have often both thought and prayed over the matter, but no benefit has accrued from their effort: they have made no real progress. They bid you to look to the Church of earlier times, and say that it was never much otherwise than it is now. What you say of the poverty and weakness of the Church in its relations to the world is true: your representation of the promise of God is glorious: all that you expect from the mighty working of the Spirit it is the highest degree desirable; *but*—it is not to be obtained. These people belong to the generation of the ten spies who were sent to spy out Canaan: the land is glorious, but the enemy in possession is too strong: we are too weak to overcome them. Lack of consecration and of

[1] Rev. iii. 17.   [2] Ezek. xxxvii. 9.

willingness to surrender everything for this blessing is the root of the unbelief, and has made them incapable of exercising the courage of Caleb when he said: "Let us go up at once, and possess it; for we are well able to overcome it."[1]

My brother, if you would be filled with the Spirit, do not suffer yourself to be held back by such reasonings. "Only believe" and strengthen yourself in the omnipotence of God. Do not say : is God able? Say rather : God is ABLE. The God who was able to raise Christ from the dead is still mighty in the midst of His people, and is able to reveal His divine life with power in your heart. Hear His voice saying to you as to Abraham: "I am God Almighty: walk thou before My face and be perfect."[2] Set your heart without distraction on what God has said that He will do, and then on the Omnipotence which is prepared to bring the promise to accomplishment. Pray to the Father that He would grant unto you to be strengthened with might by His Spirit. Adore Him who is able to do for us exceeding abundantly above all that we ask and think, and give Him the glory. Let faith in the Omnipotence of God fill your soul and you will be full of the assurance that, however difficult, however improbable, however impossible it may seem, God can fill us with His Spirit. "Only believe."

III

Although everything in you appears entirely unfit for this blessing and unworthy of it, still: "only believe."

When one prays for this blessing of being filled with

---

[1] Num. xiii. 30.   [2] Gen. xvii. 1.

the Spirit, the thought will spring up unbidden, of what one's life as a Christian has already been. The believer thinks of all the workings of divine grace in his heart, and of the incessant strivings of the Spirit. He thinks of all his efforts and prayers, of his past attempts at entire surrender and the appropriation of faith. He then looks upon what he is at the moment, upon his unfaithfulness and sin and helplessness, and he becomes dispirited. In the lapse of so many years so little progress has been made. The past testifies only of failure and unfaithfulness. What avails it to think that the future will be any better? If all his praying and believing of earlier days have been of so little avail, why should he now dare to hope that everything is to be transformed at once? He presents to himself the life of a man full of the Holy Spirit, and alongside it he sets his own life as he has learned to know it, and it becomes impossible for him to imagine that he shall ever be able to live as a man full of the Spirit. For such a task he is once for all unfit, and feels no courage to make the attempt.

Christian, when such thoughts as these throng in upon you there is but one counsel to follow, and that is: "only believe." Cast yourself into the arms of your Father who gives His children the Holy Spirit much more readily than an earthly father gives bread. Only believe, and count upon THE LOVE OF GOD. All your self-dedication and surrender, all your faith and integrity is not a work by which you have to move God or make Him willing to bless you. Far from it. It is God that desires to bless you, and that will Himself work everything in you. *God loves you as a father* and sees that, to be able to live in perfect health and happiness as His child, you have need of nothing but this one thing—to be full of His Spirit. Jesus has by His blood opened up the way to the full enjoyment of this love. You must learn to enter into this love, to abide in this love, and by faith to acknowledge that it shines upon you and surrounds you, even as the light of the sun illumines and animates your body. Begin to trust this love. I do not say in its willingness: no—in its unspeakable longing to fill you entirely with itself. It is your Father, whose love waits to make you full of His Spirit. He Himself will do it for you.

And what does he crave at your hands? Simply this, that you yield yourself to Him in utter unworthiness, nothingness, and impotence, to let Him do this work in you. He is prepared to take charge of all the preparatory work. You may be sure that He will help you by His Spirit. He will strengthen you with might in the inner man, silently and hiddenly, yet none the less surely, to abandon everything that has to be given up and to receive this treasure. He will help you in the faith of appropriation to rest in His word and to wait for Him; and He will hold Himself responsible for all the future. He will make provision that you shall be able to walk in the fulness of this blessing.

You have perhaps already formed a very high idea of what a man must be that is filled with the Spirit of God, and you see no chance of your being able to live in such a fashion. Or it may be that you have not been able to form any idea of it whatever, and are on that account afraid to strive for a life which is so unknown to you. O Christian, abandon all such thoughts. The Spirit alone, when He is once in you, will Himself teach you what that life is, for He will work it in you. God will take upon

Himself the responsibility of making you full of the Spirit, not as a treasure which *you* must carry and keep, but as a power which is to carry and keep you. Therefore, O Soul, "only believe": count upon THE LOVE OF YOUR FATHER.

In His promise of the blessing and the power of the Spirit the Lord Jesus always pointed to God the Father. He called it "the promise of the Father."[1] He directed us to the faithfulness of God: "He is faithful that promised."[2] He directed us to the power of God: the Spirit was, as power from on high, to come from God Himself.[3] He directed us to the love of God: it is as a Father that God is to give this boon to His children. Let every thought of this blessing and every desire for it only lead us to God. Here is something that HE must do, that HE must give, that HE, HE ALONE, must work. Let us in silent adoration set our heart upon God: He will do something for us. Let us joyfully trust in Him: He is able to do above all praying and thinking. His love will, O so willingly, bestow upon us a full blessing. Therefore, "only believe": God will make me full of the Spirit. And say humbly: *Behold the servant of the Lord. Let Him do to me what is good in His sight. Be it unto me according to Thy word.*[4] "Faithful is He that calleth you, WHO ALSO WILL DO IT."

---

[1] Luke xxiv. 49   [2] Heb. x. 23
[3] Acts i. 8   [4] Luke i. 38.

CHAPTER XI

HOW IT IS TO BE FOUND BY ALL

"And I will sprinkle clean water upon you, and ye shall be clean: from all your filthiness, and from all your idols, will I cleanse you. And I will put My Spirit within you, and cause you to walk in My statutes, and ye shall keep My judgments, and do them."—Ezek. xxxvi. 25, 27.

THE full Pentecostal blessing is for all the children of God. *As many* as are led by the Spirit of God, they are the children of God.[1] God does not give a half portion to any one of His children. To every one He says: "Son, thou art ever with Me, and *all that I have is thine.*"[2] Christ is not divided; he that receives Him receives Him in all His fulness. Every Christian is destined by God, and is actually called, to be filled with the Spirit.

In the preceding chapters I have had in view especially those who are to some extent acquainted with these things, and have been already in search of the truth: such as have been already led after conversion to make a more complete renunciation of sin, and to yield themselves wholly to the Lord. But it is quite conceivable that amongst those who read this book there may be Christians who have heard but little of the full Pentecostal blessing, and in whose hearts the desire has arisen to obtain a share in it. There is, however, so much that they do not as yet understand,

[1] Rom. viii. 14.　　　　　　　　[2] Luke xv. 31.

108

that they are willing indeed to have pointed out to them in the simplest possible fashion, where they are to begin, and what they have to do, in order to succeed in their desire. They are prepared to acknowledge that their life is full of sin, and that it seems to them as if they would have to strive long and earnestly, ere they can become full of the Spirit. I should like much to inspire them with fresh courage and to direct them to the God who has said: "I the Lord will hasten it in its time."[1] I should like to take them and guide them to the place where God will bless them, and to point to them out of His Word what the disposition and the attitude must be in which they can receive this blessing.

I

First of all, there must be a new discovery and confession and casting away of sin.

In the message of Ezekiel, God first promised: "I will cleanse you," and then: "I will put My Spirit within you." A vessel into which anything precious is to be poured must always first be cleansed. So, if the Lord is to give you a new and full blessing, a new cleansing must also take place. In your conversion, it is true, there was a confession and putting away of sin. Yet this separation was but superficial and external. The soul was still half enveloped in darkness: it thought more of its heinous sins and the punishment they might entail. After conversion it did indeed endeavour to overcome sin, but the effort did not succeed. It did not know in what holiness the Lord desires

[1] Isa. ix. 22 (R.V.).

His people to live: it did not know how pure and holy the Lord would have it be and would make it be.

This new cleansing must come through new confession and discovery of sin. The old leaven cannot be purged away unless it be first searched for and found. Do not say that you already know sufficiently well that your Christian life is full of sin. Sit down in silent meditation and with the express purpose of seeing of what sort your life as a Christian has been. How much pride, self-seeking, worldliness, self-will, and impurity has been in it. Can such a heart receive the fulness of the Spirit? It is impossible. Look into your home life. In your intercourse with wife and children, servants and friends, do not hastiness of temper, anxiety about yourself, bitterness, idle or harsh or unbecoming words testify how little you have been cleansed? Look into the current life of the Church. How much religion is there that is merely intellectual, or formal, or pleasing to men, without that real humiliation of spirit, that real desire for the living God, that real love for Jesus, that real subjection to the Word, which constitute worship in spirit and in truth. Look into your general course of conduct. Consider whether the people amongst whom you mingle can testify that they have observed, by your honourable spirit and disinterestedness and freedom from worldly-mindedness, that you are one who has been cleansed from sin by God. Contemplate all this in the light of what God expects from you and has offered to work in you, and take your place as a guilty, helpless soul that must be cleansed before God can bestow the full blessing upon you.

On the back of this discovery follows the actual putting

away and casting out of what is impure. This is something that you are simply bound to do. You must come with these sins, and especially with those that are most strictly your own besetting sins, and acknowledge them before God in confession, and there and then make renunciation of them. You must be brought to the conviction that your life is a guilty and shameful life. You are not at liberty to take comfort from the consideration that you are so weak, or that the majority of Christians live no higher life. It must become a matter of earnest resolve with you that your life is to undergo a complete transformation. The sins that still cleave to you are to be cast off and done away with.

Perhaps you may say in reply that you find yourself unable to do away with them or cast them off. I tell you that you are quite able to do this; and in this way. You can give these sins up to God. If there should happen to be anything in my house that I wish to have taken away, and that I myself am unable to carry, I call for men who shall do it for me, and I give it over into their hands, saying: "Look here: take that away," and they do it. So I am able to say that I have put away this thing out of my house. In like manner you can give up to God those sins of yours, against which you feel yourself utterly impotent. You can give them up to Him to be dealt with as He desires and He will fulfil His promise: "I will cleanse you from all your filthiness." There is nothing so needful as that there should be a very definite understanding between you and the Lord, that you on your part really confess your sin and bid it everlasting farewell and give it up, and that you wait on Him until

He assures you that He has taken it, or rather has taken your heart and life, into His own hands to give you a complete victory.

II

In this way you come to a new discovery, and reception, and experience of what Christ is and is prepared to do for you.

If the knowledge of sin at conversion is superficial, so also is the faith in Jesus. Our faith, our reception of Jesus never goes further or deeper than our insight into sin. If since your conversion you have learned to know the inward invincible power of sin in you, you are now prepared to receive from God a discovery of the inward invincible power of the Lord Jesus in your heart, such as you have hitherto had no idea of. If you really long for a complete deliverance from sin, so as to be able to live in obedience to God, God will reveal the Lord Jesus to you as a complete Saviour. He will make you know that, although the flesh always remains in you, with its inclination to evil, the Lord Jesus will so dwell in your heart that the power of the flesh shall be kept in subjection by Him, in order that you may no longer do the will of the flesh. Through Jesus Christ, God will cleanse you from all unrighteousness, so that day by day you may walk before God with a pure heart. What you really need is the discovery that He is prepared to work this change in you, and that you may receive it by faith, here and now.

Yes: this is what Jesus Christ desires to work in you by the Holy Spirit. He came to put away sin; not the guilt and punishment of it only, but sin itself. He has not only mastered the power and dominion of the law and its curse over you, but has also completely broken and taken away the power and dominion of sin. He has completely rescued you as a new-born soul from beneath the power of sin; and He lives in His heavenly authority and all-pervading presence in order to work out this deliverance in you. In this power He will live in you and Himself carry out His work in you. As the indwelling Christ, He is bent on maintaining and manifesting His redemption in you. The sins which you have confessed, the pride and the lovelessness, the worldly-mindedness and vanity and all uncleanness, He will by His power take out of your heart; so that, although the flesh may tempt you, the choice and the joy of your heart abide in Him and in His obedience to God's will. Yes: you may indeed become "more than conqueror" through Him that loved you.[1] As the indwelling Christ, He will overcome sin in you.

What then is required on our side? Only this, a thing that can be done at once, namely, that when the soul sees it to be true that Jesus will carry out this work, it shall then open the door before Him and receive Him into the heart as Lord and King. Yes: that can be done at once. A house that has remained closely shut for twenty years can be penetrated by the light in a moment, if the doors and windows are thrown open. In like manner, a heart that has remained enveloped in darkness and impotence for twenty years, because it knew not that Jesus was willing to take the victory over sin into His own hands, can have its whole experience changed in a

[1] Rom. viii. 37.

moment. When it acknowledges its sinful condition and yields itself to God, and believes that the Son of God is prepared to assume the responsibility of the inner life and its purification from sin; when it ventures to trust the Lord that He will do this work at the very moment; then it may firmly believe that it is done, and that Jesus takes all that is in me into His own hands.

This is indeed an act of faith, that must be held fast in faith. When doors and windows are thrown open, and the light streaming in drives out the darkness, we discover at once how much dust and impurity there is in the house. But the light shines just in order that we may see how to take it away. When we receive Christ into the heart everything is not yet perfected: light and gladness are not seen and experienced at once; but by faith the soul knows that He who is faithful will keep His word and will surely do His work. The faith that has up to this moment only sought and wrestled, now rests in the Lord and His Word. *It knows that what was begun by faith must be carried forward only by faith.* It says: "I abide in Jesus; I know that He abides in me and that He will manifest Himself unto me." As Jesus cleansed the lepers with a word, and it was only when they were on their way to the priest that they found out they were clean, so He cleanses us by His Word. He that firmly holds that fact in faith will see the proofs of it.

III

So the soul is prepared to receive the full blessing of *the Spirit*.

The Lord gave first the promise, *I will cleanse you*; and then the second promise, *I will put My Spirit within you.* The Holy Spirit cannot come with power or fill the heart and continue to dwell in it, unless a special and complete cleansing first takes place within it. The Spirit and sin are engaged in a mortal combat. The only reason why the Spirit works so feebly in the Church is sin, which is all too little known or dreaded or cast out. Men do not believe in the power of Christ to cleanse; and therefore He cannot do His work of baptizing with the Spirit. It is from Christ that the Spirit comes, and to Christ the Spirit returns again. It is the heart that gives Christ liberty to exercise dominion in it that shall inherit the full blessing. Therefore my reader, if you have understood the lesson of this chapter, and have done what has been suggested to you; if you have believed in Jesus as the Lord that cleanses you and dwells in you to keep you clean, be assured that God will certainly fulfil His word : "I will cleanse you *and put My Spirit within you.*" Cleave to Jesus, who cleanses you: let Him be all within you; God will see to it that you are filled with the Spirit.

Only keep in view these two truths.

First, that the gift and the blessing and the fulness of the Spirit do not always come, as on the day of Pentecost, with external observation. God is often a God that hideth Himself: do not be surprised, therefore, if your heart does not at once feel, as you should like it to feel, immediately after your act of surrender or appropriation. Rest assured that, if you fully trust Christ to do everything for you, He there and then begins to do it in secret by His Spirit. Count upon it that, if you present yourself to God as a pure vessel, cleansed by Christ, to be filled with the Spirit, God will take you at your word and say unto you : "Receive ye the Holy Spirit; be it unto you according to your faith."[1] At that moment bow down before Him, more and more silently, more and more deeply, in holy adoration and expectation, in the blessed assurance that the unseen God has now begun to carry on His work more mightily in you, and that He will also manifest it to you more gloriously than ever before.

The other thing you must keep in view is the purpose for which the Spirit is given. I will put My Spirit within you, and *I will cause you to walk in My statutes and to keep My judgments and do them.* The fulness of the Spirit must be sought and received and kept with the direct aim that you shall now simply and wholly live to do God's will and work upon the earth,—yes: only to be able to live like the Lord Jesus, and to say with Him: "Lo! I come to do Thy will."[2] If you cherish this disposition, the fulness of the Spirit may be positively expected. Be full of courage and yield yourself to walk in God's statutes and to keep His judgments and do them, and you may trust God to keep His word that *He will cause you* to keep and do them. He, the living God, will work in you. Even before you are aware how the Spirit is in you, He will enable you to experience the full blessing.

My brother, have you never yet known the fulness of the Spirit, or have you perhaps been really seeking it for a long while without finding it? Here you have at last the sure method of winning it. Acknowledge the sinfulness of your condition as a Christian and make renunciation of it,

---

[1] John xx. 22.   [2] Psa. xl. 7, 8; Heb. x. 7.

once and for all, by yielding it up to God. Acknowledge that the Lord Jesus is ready and able to cleanse your heart from its sin; to conquer these sins by His entrance into it, and to set you free; and that His purpose is to do this at once. Take Him now as your Lord, at once and for ever. Then you may be assured that God will put His Spirit within you in a way and a measure and a power of which you have hitherto had no idea. Be assured that He will do it. O permit Him to begin; let Him do it in you now. Amen.

CHAPTER XII

HOW EVERYTHING MUST BE GIVEN UP FOR IT

"Then shall the Son also Himself be subjected to Him that did subject all things unto Him, that God may be all in all."—1 Cor. xv. 28.

WHEN we speak of entire consecration, we are frequently asked what the precise distinction is betwixt the ordinary doctrine of sanctification, and the preaching of that gracious work which has begun to prevail in the Church in recent years. One answer that may be given is that the distinction lies solely in the little word, *all.* That word is the key of the secret. The ordinary method of proclaiming the necessity of holiness is true so far as it goes; but sufficient emphasis is not laid on this one point of the "All." So is it also with the question as to the reasons why the fulness of the Spirit is not more widely enjoyed. That little word "All" suggests the explanation. So long as the "All" of God, of sin, of Christ, of surrender, of the Spirit, and of faith, is not fully understood, the soul cannot enjoy all that God desires to give and be, all that God would have it be. In this our last meditation let us consider the full Pentecostal blessing from this standpoint. We would fain do this in a spirit of humble waiting on God, and with the prayer that He would make us by His Spirit feel so deeply where the evil lies and what the remedy is, that we shall be ready to give up everything in order to receive nothing less than everything.

I

THE ALL OF GOD

It lies in the very being and nature of God that He must be all. From Him and through Him and to Him are all things. As God He is the life of everything: all life is only the effect of His direct and continuous operation. It is because all is thus through Him and from Him that it is also to Him. Everything that exists serves only as a means for the manifestation of the goodness and wisdom and power of God.

Sin consists in nothing but this, that man determined to be something and would not suffer God to be everything; and the redemption of Jesus has no other aim than that God should again become everything in our heart and life. At the end, even the Son shall be subjected to the Father, that God may be all in all. Nothing less than this is what redemption is to secure. Christ Himself has shown in His life what it means to be nothing, and to suffer God to be everything; and as He once lived upon the earth, so does He still live in the hearts of His people. According to the measure in which they receive and rejoice in the truth that God is all, will the fulness of the blessing be able to find it's way into their life.

The All of God: that is what we must seek. In His will, His honour, His power must He be everything for us. No movement of our time, no word of our lips, no movement of our heart, no satisfying of the needs of our physical life, should there be that is not the expression of the will, the glory, the power of God. Only the man who discerns this and consents to it, who desires and seeks after it, who believes and appropriates it, can rightly understand what the fulness of the Spirit must effect, and why it is necessary that we should forsake everything if we desire to obtain it. God must be not merely *something*, not merely *much*, but literally, *all*.

II

THE ALL OF SIN

What is sin? It is the absence of God; separation from God. Where man is guided by his own will, his own honour, his own power; where the will, the honour, the operation of God are not manifested, there sin must be at work. Sin is death and misery, only because it is a turning away from God to the creature.

Sin is in no sense a thing that may exist in man along with other things that are good. No: as God was once everything, so has sin in fallen man become everything. It now dominates and penetrates his whole being, even as God should have been allowed to do. His nature in every part of it is corrupt. We still have our natural existence in God, and doubtless with not a few good inclinations in nature and character, just as these are to be found in the lower creatures. But of what is *good* in the spiritual and heavenly sense of the word, of what is done out of inward harmony with God or the direction of His Spirit—of all this there is nothing that has its origin in His nature. All is in sin, and under the influence of sin.

The All of sin: some small measure of the knowledge of this fact was necessary even at the time of conversion. This, however, was still very imperfect. If a Christian is to make progress and become fully convinced of the necessity of being filled with the Spirit, his eyes must be opened to the extent in which sin dominates over everything within him. Everything in him is tainted with sin, his will, his power, his heart; and therefore the omnipotence of God must take in hand the renewal of everything by the Holy Spirit. Man is utterly impotent to that which is good in the highest sense: he can do no more of what is good than what the Spirit actually works in him at any moment. He learns also to see the All of sin just as distinctly in the world around him; for the fairest, the most useful, and the most legitimate possessions or enjoyments are all under the power of sin. Everything must be sacrificed and given over to death: the All of God must expel the All of sin. God must again live wholly and entirely within us, and take inwardly and continuously the place which sin usurped. He that desires this change will rightly understand and desire the fulness of the Spirit, and as he believes will certainly receive it.

III

THE ALL OF CHRIST

The Son is the revelation of the Father: the All of God is exhibited to our view and made accessible to us in the Son. On this account the ALL of Christ is just as necessary and infinite as that of God. Christ is God come upon the earth to undo the All of sin, to win back and restore in man the lost All of God. To this end we must know thoroughly the All of Christ.

The idea which most believing disciples have of the All of Christ is that He alone does everything in the atonement and the forgiveness of sin. This is indeed the glorious beginning of His redemptive work, but still only the beginning. God has given in Him all that we have need of: life and all grace. Christ Himself desires to be our life and strength, the Indweller of our heart, who animates that heart and makes it what it ought to be before God. To know the All of Christ, and to understand how intensely and how completely and how really Christ is prepared to be everything in us, is the secret of true sanctification. He that discerns the will of God in this principle and from the heart yields himself to its operation has found the pathway to the full blessing of Pentecost.

The All of Christ. Acknowledge this in humble joyful thanksgiving: confess that everything has been given by God in Him. Receive with firm confidence the fact that Christ is all and the promise that He will work all, yes, *all*, in you. Consent from the heart that this must be so, and confirm it by laying everything at His feet and offering it up to Him. The two things go together: let Him be and do all; let Him reign and rule over all. Let there be nothing in which He does not rule and operate. It is not impossible for you to accomplish this change. Let Him be everything; let Him have everything, in order that by His Almighty energy He may fill everything with Himself.

IV

THE ALL OF SURRENDER

Leave all, sell all, forsake all: that was the Lord's requirement when He was here on earth: the requirement is in force still.

The discernment of the fact that Christ is all leads of itself to the acknowledgment that He must have all. The chief hindrance of the Christian life is that, because men do not believe that Christ is all, they consequently never think of the necessity of giving Him all.

Everything must be given to Him, because everything is under sin. He cannot cleanse and keep a thing when it is not so yielded up to Him that He can take full possession of it and fill it. All must be given up to Him, because He alone can bring *the all of God* to its rightful supremacy within us. Even what appears useful or lawful or innocent becomes defiled by the stain of our selfishness when it is held fast in our own possession and for our own enjoyment. We must surrender it into the hands and the power of Christ: only there can it be sanctified.

The All of surrender: O it is because Christians are so ignorant of the requirement that all their praying and hearing avail so little. If then, O Soul, you are really prepared to turn to God for the fulness of the Spirit; if you have turned to Christ to have your heart purified and kept pure; then be assured that it is your blessed privilege to regard and deal with everything—everything that you have to strive for or do as given up to Him. The All of surrender will be the measure of your experience of the All of Christ. In a preceding chapter we have seen that surrender may be carried out at once and as a whole: let us not merely read and think of this, but actually do it. Yes: this very day, let the All of Christ be the power of a surrender on our part that shall be immediate, complete, and everlasting.

V

THE ALL OF THE SPIRIT

The All of God and the All of Christ demand as a necessary consequence the All of the Spirit. It is the work of the Spirit to glorify the Son as dwelling *in us*, and by Him to reveal the Father; how can He do this if He Himself is not All and has not All and does not possess and penetrate All with His own power? To be filled with the Spirit, to let the Spirit have All, is indispensable to a true, healthful Christian life.

It is a source of great loss in the life of Christendom to-day that the truth is not discerned, that the Three-One God must have All. Even the professing Christian oftentimes makes it his very first aim to find out what he is and what he desires, what pleases him and makes him happy. Then he brings in God in the second place to secure this happiness. The claim of God is not the primary or main consideration. He does not discern that God must have him at His disposal even in the most trivial details of his life to manifest His divine glory in him. He is not aware that this entire filling with the will and the operation of God would prove to be his highest happiness. He does not know that the very same Christ who once lived upon the earth as the obedient, lowly Servant of God, entirely surrendered to the will of the Father, is prepared to abide and work in like manner in his heart and life now. It is on this account that he can never fully comprehend how necessary it is that the Spirit must be all and must fill him completely.

O my brother, if these thoughts have had any influence with you, suffer yourself to be brought without delay to the acknowledgment that the Spirit must be all in you. Say from the heart: "I am not at liberty to make any, even the least, exception: the Spirit must have all." Then add to this confession the simple thought that Christ has come to restore the All of God; that the Spirit is given to reveal the All of Christ within us, so that God may again be all; that the love of the Father is eagerly longing to secure again His own supreme place with us; and then your heart will be filled with the sure confidence that the Father actually gives you the fulness of the Spirit.

VI

THE ALL OF FAITH

"*All things* are possible to him that believeth." "*All things* whatsoever ye pray and ask for, believe that ye have received them, and ye shall have them."[1] The preceding sections of this chapter have taught us to understand why it is that faith is all. It is because God is all. It is because man is nothing, and thus has nothing good in him except the capacity for receiving God. When he becomes a believer, that which God reveals becomes of itself a heavenly light that illumines him. He sees then what God is prepared to be for him; he keeps his soul silent before God and open to God, and gives God the opportunity of working all by

[1] Mark xi. 24 (R.V.).

the Spirit. The more unceasingly and undividedly he believes, the more fully can the All of God and Christ prevail and work in him.

The All of Faith. How little is it understood in the Church that the one and only thing I have to do is without ceasing to keep my soul in its nothingness and dependence silent and open before God, that He may be free to work in me; that faith as the willing acceptance and expectation of God's working, receives all and can achieve all. Every glance at my own impotence or sin, every glance at the promise of God and His power to fulfil it, must rouse me to the gladness of faith, to the willing, cheerful acknowledgment that God is able to work all, to the assurance that He will do it.

Let such a faith, as the act of a moment, look upon Christ even to-day and move you on the one hand to make renunciation of every known sin, and on the other to receive Him as One who purifies you, who keeps you, who dwells in your heart. O that faith might receive the All of Christ and take Him with All that He is! O that your faith might then see that the All of the Spirit is your rightful heritage, and that your hope is sure that the full blessing has been bestowed upon you by God Himself, and will be revealed in you!

O Soul, if the All of God, the All of Christ, the All of the Spirit be so immeasurable, if the dominion and power of the terrible All of sin be so unlimited, if the All of your surrender to God and your decision to live wholly for Him be also so real, then let your faith in what God will do for you be also unlimited. "He that believeth in Me, out of his heart shall flow rivers of living water."

My reader, the time has now come when we must part. Ere this takes place, let me press on your heart one thing. There is something that can be done *to-day*. As the Holy Spirit saith: "To-day, if ye will hear His voice, harden not your heart."[1] I cannot promise that you shall immediately overflow with the light and joy of the Holy Spirit. I do not promise you that you shall to-day feel very holy and truly blessed. But what can take place is this: to-day you may receive Christ as One who purifies you, and baptizes, and fills with the Spirit. ·Yes: to-day you may surrender your whole being to Him to be henceforth wholly under the mastery of the Spirit. To-day you may acknowledge and appropriate the All of the Spirit as your personal possession. To-day you may submit to the requirement of the All of faith and begin to live only and wholly in the faith of what Christ will do in you through the Spirit. This you may do; this you ought to do. Kneel down at the mercy-seat and do it. Read once more the earlier chapter with its directions as to what Christ is prepared to do, and surrender yourself this very hour as an empty vessel to be filled with the Spirit, that your whole life may be carried out under the leading of the Spirit. In His own time God will certainly accomplish it in you.

There is also something, however, that He on His part is prepared to do. To-day He is ready to give you the assurance that He accepts your surrender and to seal on your heart the conviction that the fulness of the Spirit belongs to you. O wait upon Him to give you this to-day!

My brother, pray listen to my last words. The All of God summons you. The All of sin summons you. The All

[1] Ps. xcv. 7; Heb. iii. 15.

of Christ summons you. The All of the surrender that Jesus requires summons you. The All of the Spirit, His indispensableness and His glory, summons you. The All of faith summons you. Come and let the love of God conquer you. Come and let the glorious salvation master you. Do not hark away back from the glorious tidings that the triune God, with all that He is, is prepared to be your All; but be silent and listen to it, until your soul becomes constrained to give the answer, "Even in me God shall be all." Take Christ anew to-day as One who has given His life that God may be all, and do you also yield your life for this supreme end. God will fill you also with His Holy Spirit. Amen.